# 14 NIGHTS
Learning about homelessness the hard way

# The Archer Project

## 14 NIGHTS

©2023 The Archer Project &
Meze Publishing Ltd. All rights reserved
First edition printed in 2023 in the UK
ISBN: 978-1-915538-17-8

Written by: Tim Renshaw,
James Creed-Gosling, Andrea Fowler,
Chris Lynam, Szymon Slotwinski,
Jo Leeming, Richard Allen,
Surriya Falconer

Edited by: Katie Fisher
Photography by: Mark Harvey
Cover Art by: Luke Horton
Designed by: Paul Cocker
Sales & PR: Emma Toogood & Lizzy Capps
Contributors: Phil Turner, Lis Ellis,
Sam Borland, Rhianna Emberson,
Vicky Frost, Kate McCann, Emily Retford
Printed by: Bell & Bain Ltd, UK

**meze** PUBLISHING

**FSC** MIX
Paper | Supporting
responsible forestry
FSC® C007785

Published by: Meze Publishing Limited
Unit 1b, 2 Kelham Square
Kelham Riverside
Sheffield S3 8SD
Web: www.mezepublishing.co.uk
Telephone: 0114 275 7709
Email: info@mezepublishing.co.uk

No part of this book shall be reproduced
or transmitted in any form or by any
means, electronic or mechanical,
including photocopying, recording, or by
any information retrieval system without
written permission of the publisher.

Although every precaution has been
taken in the preparation of this work,
the publisher and author assume no
responsibility for errors or omissions.
Neither is any liability assumed for
damages resulting from the use of this
information contained herein.

# Foreword
# By Dame Julie Kenny

I was first introduced to The Archer Project in 2012, when I had the privilege of serving breakfasts to their guests and having the opportunity to speak to some of those people about their hopes and aspirations and what they thought of the project. Of course, not everyone took the time to speak with me but those who did were already on the journey to a renewed life and possibly a new home.

The Archer Project changes lives; that is why I support it and why I accepted the honour of writing the foreword for this book. For over 30 years, The Archer Project has provided a vital service for the city of Sheffield and its homeless citizens, and yet their work is non-stop and in these challenging times the number of homeless people on our streets is not reducing.

Homelessness is not always something you are randomly dealt; it is brought about by a variety of circumstances. Some of these may stem from childhood and traumatic experiences you may be trying to escape, or trauma in your life right now. Perhaps you find yourself unemployed or divorced... whatever the story, one thing you can be sure of is that each individual will have suffered more than enough before they get to the street.

Last year, CEO of The Archer Project Tim Renshaw spent a fortnight living and sleeping out to shine a light on the plight of the homeless. He had a tent and a sleeping bag for those 14 nights, which many homeless people do not. I remember reading his blogs each day; I was captivated by them, horrified by some of his thoughts and experiences, and very concerned as to Tim's mental health which appeared to decline in such a short time while he lived the same life as the people he works with. Tim knew he had to endure homelessness for 14 days, but for the homeless there is no end date. This is why The Archer Project is so vital. Every individual deserves the chance of a home, health and happiness. A new beginning.

By reading this book – both Tim's blogs and the contributions of those who have come through the project – you will come to better understand the plight of the homeless, and how The Archer Project is much more than serving breakfast, providing showers and clean clothes, or facilitating medical help. It is about engaging with every person who walks through their doors, so they can feel listened to in a stable environment that they can return to on a regular basis. It's about creating a space to help these individuals find their way to a much better life.

# Contents

Foreword By Dame Julie Kenny ... 4
Welcome to The Archer Project
By James Creed-Gosling ... 10
Introduction By Tim Renshaw ... 14

## Tim's Blog

**Day One:** Starting Out ... 20
**Day Two:**
If only I could carry a mattress! ... 24
**Day Three:** Can I trust you? ... 28
**Day Four:** The Haves and Have Nots ... 32
**Day Five (a):** I don't want to
seem ungrateful, but... ... 36
**Day Five (b):**
"Tim, you look like s##t." ... 38
**Day Six:** It really is beyond belief ... 42
**Day Seven:** Rain, rain, go away... ... 46
**Day Eight:** And still it goes on... ... 50
**Day Nine:** What If? ... 54
**Day Ten:** I want to be where you are ... 58
**Day Eleven:** Lest We Forget ... 62
**Day Twelve:** It's Everywhere ... 66
**Day Thirteen:**
First survive, then thrive ... 70
**Day Fourteen:** The Loo ... 74
**Day Fifteen:** Has it ended yet? ... 78
**Afterthoughts 1:**
Down but not out ... 82
**Afterthoughts 2:**
Health and Wellbeing ... 84
**Afterthoughts 3:**
Female Homelessness ... 86

## Reflection

F##k You! ... 90
James Creed-Gosling ... 96
Jo Leeming ... 100
Szymon Slotwinski ... 102
Andrea Fowler ... 106
Chris Lynam ... 108
Richard Allen ... 110
Carrie ... 112
Volunteering with The Archer Project
By Surriya Falconer ... 116
Better Together By Tim Renshaw ... 120
Acknowledgements ... 124

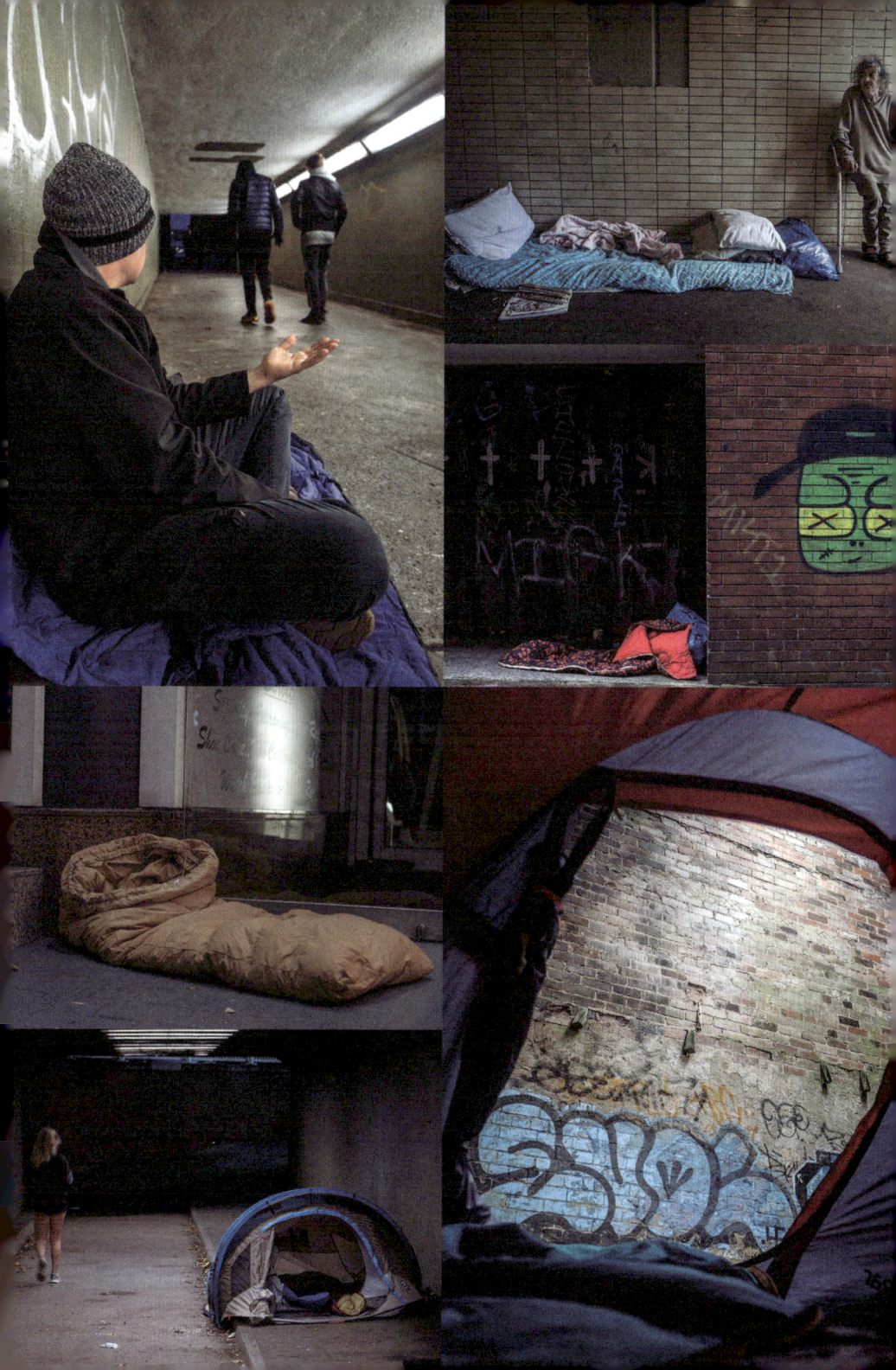

# Welcome to The Archer Project
# By James Creed-Gosling

I would like to tell you about The Archer Project. I used the project for two years while sofa-surfing following a long period of rough sleeping, at a desperately low point in my life. Initially I came for the practical help I needed. A shower and a hot meal. A place to come and do my washing. It was for me, as it is for many others, an anchor point in an otherwise drifting existence. A busy, noisy, sometimes overwhelming place where you are welcomed in to step off the not-so merry-go-round lifestyle of having no fixed abode. It's a world within the world.

The practical support The Archer Project provides is so important to the day-to-day survival of the homeless community. From housing support to hot meals, showers and clothing, doctors and dentists, these things are essential. Survival is one thing, but everyone has the right to do more than merely survive. People deserve to thrive. We all need to be listened to and to know that someone cares. I was listened to, I had real conversations with people, and I found validation that my situation was real and there was a way out of it. I was offered support from the project and, through them, from other important agencies that helped me find my way through the daunting maze of rebuilding my life.

Those real conversations are key to the work of The Archer Project. Often, they are the only interactions a rough sleeper may have for the whole day. They are a source of hope and encouragement; they led me to a sense of purpose. Yes, I needed a home and other practical stuff but without a sense of purpose I wouldn't have taken the steps I have done, and I might still be facing the daily trudge of a life of addiction flirting with homelessness. Conversations are the building blocks of a future beyond mere existence, isolation and disconnection.

So, digging a little deeper, that is what The Archer Project really offers. The team understands about the myriad traumas a person has experienced that led them to the street. Every person's story is different, of course, but unless you start by expecting a level of dysfunction where lives have been shaped by abuse and neglect or tragedy, then you won't get to the starting point of acceptance that I needed. That trauma never really goes away but it can be dealt with or managed so that it doesn't ruin all of life's opportunities. Through The Archer Project I got to talk about my traumas, I was understood, and eventually that meant my confidence and self-esteem grew. The project believed in me. Self-belief, so alien to so many people who suffer homelessness, started to become a reality.

So where does that leave me today? I'm far from homeless! I was offered paid supported work through The Archer Project's social enterprise arm, and I took it. Actually, I grasped it. It has changed my life. The aim of the work I do is to enable people to become independent enough to thrive through employment and a fulfilling, balanced life. I faced all the stuff that many of those people face today, and I help them deal with it. What more could I ask for?

With support, time, patience, and belief people can recognise and fulfil the potential that many have never previously recognised in themselves. This was my experience and The Archer Project have believed in me every step of the way, even when I didn't believe in myself. I love this place and all its people and the work we do. Yes, I work here now! I am immensely proud to be a part of the transitions and the triumphs of everyone who comes through the doors of this wonderful place. Proud to be able to do my small part to repay what I was given so kindly, which saved my life.

# Introduction
# By Tim Renshaw

Chris, one of the writers of this book, walked through one of Sheffield's underpasses past two men, smartly dressed and peeing against the wall, a stream of urine beginning to flow in the direction of a man sat on his sleeping bag, fallen slightly forward, as if dozing. One of the men said to the other, "Look at that f#####g smackhead."

I hope I don't need to point out the irony.

In that brief moment, there is so much of the misunderstanding and judgement that this book speaks against. The man on his sleeping bag, the 'smackhead', has a name. He most likely has a history of being abused or neglected, a history that shaped his childhood and teenage years and helped form his adult behaviours. He is probably a survivor with an ability to get through the worst of days and nights that most of us would be terrified of. He will survive being soaked in the urine of those two 'superior' men, out in the city having a good time.

He will wake up and curse his bad luck. More likely than not he will feel depressed and alone, as if the world doesn't care. But he will get up and carry on. It is also possible that at some point he will decide that life just isn't worth it, or he may contract an illness as the result of the life he has lived and die relatively young or, like Chris himself, he might meet the person or organisation – like The Archer Project – who provides the support to help him achieve the life he dreams of. It will be a slow process and the memories from childhood and the street will never leave him, but they will be outweighed by his success and the memories that creates.

The story of homelessness is the story of individual people who have suffered more than enough before they get to the street. The street just makes life a whole lot worse.

In this book I tell of an incident on the last day of my sleepout when I walked past a shop that I wanted to go into because I felt judged by someone who looked at me. Afterwards it struck me that had I been properly homeless for more than 14 nights, I would probably have responded differently. I recalled a story that a woman we will call B recounted to me, about when another woman looked at her as she searched through a bin looking for tab ends to make a roll up cigarette. B wasn't proud that bins were her last hope. She wasn't proud to be on the street. She felt judged. She is also a fearsome, wonderful woman who won't be put down. I can't remember the precise words she flung at the woman watching her, but it amounted to a less polite version of "leave me alone, don't stare, you don't know how lucky you are."

I imagine others looked on and judged her for what she said too. It is her behaviour that is seen as offensive rather than our judgement, just as it is the 'smackhead' who is ruining the city environment rather than the two well-dressed men urinating in public. Hopefully what follows will change your mind. But let me be clear about what it is that I am hoping for; instead of judging the behaviours of people on the street, or even their presence, we should start to judge the causes, the reasons these people's lives have become so impoverished. If our children don't experience extended traumas, they will have opportunities instead of nightmares. And if we can intervene when trauma does happen, we might stop, or at least reduce, the decline that leads to the streets.

Before, during and after my 14-night sleepout I was aware that my attempt was fake. I haven't disguised that and I don't apologise for it. How could it be anything else? The joy of turning my blog into a book has been in talking to those who slept on the streets because they had to. I sat down one morning to listen to one of those people and he smiled before he said, "I was talking about your blogs to some friends yesterday (two other former rough sleepers) and we want to say well done. But you know you didn't have to raise the money for drugs during the day, don't you? And when you kept thinking of your house, it was because you had one to think about. But well done! We mean that, seriously." I laughed and accepted the compliment.

We all have personal heroes, people we admire because of what they have done and achieved. I am deadly serious when I say I work with some of the people I think of as heroes. They have tackled addictions and won, built new lives at the same time as carrying and dealing with stigmas of the past. What's more, they tell me, a part of every day is summoning the determination to remain on track, to remain clean and to live the new life.

The stories of real rough sleepers are shocking and that's why it is important to include them. They take us further into homelessness than my blogs ever could do and I'm grateful to them for sharing their stories with us.

# DAY ONE

# STARTING OUT

# Day One: Starting Out

I've said goodbye to home for the next 14 days. My bed, the kettle, TV, radio, microwave, fridge, and even my car have been left behind. Oh, I forgot the shower and toilet. I have got my toothbrush though!

This morning, people at Sheffield Cathedral Church wished me well, prayed over me, told me to stay safe and to be careful. I have no intention of not being careful and I know this sleepout is to genuine rough sleeping what glamping is to trekking in the Himalayas. There is a world of difference.

I have chosen to sleep rough and prepared for it. I walked away from home already equipped with a sleeping bag and tent. Having both is not unknown for rough sleepers but having them on your first night of sleeping rough is. By rights, I should have to do at least one night with nothing, unable to sleep and, at this time of year, probably walking around to stay warm when it comes to the coldest part of the night at about 3am.

There are so many differences between my sleepout and genuine homelessness, but when I was talking to a few people who are former rough sleepers they told me not to worry, I would learn enough! That's what I hope. It's started already: where do I go now? What do I do? There's a lot of hours between now and bedtime. I've given up family life, I have no one to speak to, in a busy city centre I feel alone and with a rucksack on my back and dressed for the worst weather, I don't fit in. It's a weird feeling.

> **I've given up family life, I have no one to speak to, in a busy city centre I feel alone and with a rucksack on my back and dressed for the worst weather, I don't fit in.**

## Day Two: If only I could carry a mattress!

And a pillow, that would be nice. My inch-thick self-inflating mattress was better than nothing; it kept me insulated but I never really got comfortable for very long.

Last night was my first of 14 nights sleeping rough. I was out at Mosborough, welcomed by St Mark's Church with enough sandwiches for tea and breakfast, but by 5pm I was on my own. I sat on a concrete slab and wondered what I was supposed to do now. By 6pm, I'd laid my sleeping bag out and rearranged it three or four times. I thought about food because there was a chip shop across the road from the church. I wasn't hungry but eating is doing something, and I was restless.

At 7.30pm, I woke up having dozed off, which was a relief – I'd been able to forget about being alone and potentially vulnerable enough to fall asleep. The noises around me had changed and it was darker. The road was quieter and sudden sounds of people talking grabbed my attention, so I kept sitting up to see if anyone was in the churchyard. They weren't, and no one seemed interested in me, thank goodness.

It can't have bothered me too much because at 9pm a voice saying "Hi, are you okay?" woke me with a start. Fortunately, it was a familiar face. H is a loner; he is a rough sleeper but, by and large, he tries to avoid other rough sleepers, especially at night. He sat down with his two-litre bottle of cider. He'd travelled from the city centre, 'jumping' the tram, to keep me company and for the next three hours we talked. He started by asking why I wasn't going the whole hog and drinking eight pints of special brew or whatever else, because using something to cope, to forget, is part of the deal. I told him what he already knew,

that I wasn't the real deal. As if to make me more aware of that, he got up and went to the street to blag a cigarette and came back delighted with three good tab ends and a single complete cigarette.

I'm not sure how long it will take before I am desperate for alcohol or something else to numb the experience of having no place to call my home. I hope it is more than 14 days. I don't smoke but if I did, the desperation for a cigarette would make me blag them very soon, and maybe collecting tab ends would follow. I do know that after wondering what to do and how to pass the time, I really enjoyed having company.

When the clock had struck midnight, with just one litre of cider gone, he lay down and was snoring within five minutes. Hardened to life without a mattress, he was snoring every time I woke to change positions and pull my makeshift pillow back into a pile. He was still asleep when I got up at 6.30am to leave. I heard him say goodbye and wish me well for the rest of my journey. He may never know how he made the start of it so much more palatable.

**Last night was my first of 14 nights sleeping rough.**

# DAY THREE

# CAN I TRUST YOU?

# Day Three: Can I trust you?

I spent the first part of last night scanning the people passing by me. They were taking a short cut through St Aidan's churchyard and walked right next to me, tucked up in the doorway. It's the closest I want to be to feeling afraid.

A man walked past and noticed me. Immediately, he looked straight ahead, avoiding any eye contact. What was I? Something to be afraid of? Something unwanted? I didn't know but I instantly felt wary of him. Another did the same. The first man returned, eyes fixed away from me. A man and a woman walked by; the woman turned, looked surprised to see me and then smiled and said hello. What a smile, such a small but valuable thing.

I'd started to feel vulnerable and question whether I was safe. In just half an hour I'd realised that I needed to stay alert. I wasn't going to take my shoes off in case I needed to get up quickly. I was going to drape my sleeping bag over me instead of getting in it. I sat up so I didn't look like I was sleeping, as if that made me safer.

That smile and the 'hello' didn't change my plans, but it did do something. I was recognised. I was okay enough for someone to speak to me.

A man came by and stopped just past where I was sitting. He'd noticed me but stood looking the other way. He wandered back to the other side of the doorway and did the same. He just stood there, looking up and down the road. There seemed no earthly reason for anybody to stop either side of that doorway, never mind both. What was he doing? Was it time to get up and move? What does someone with bad intentions look like? I was glad I'd kept my shoes on.

The man was smoking; he turned and looked at me and said, "Do you want one?"

"No, thank you, I don't smoke," I replied.

"I shouldn't be smoking. I'm just out of sight of my wife here, so I can smoke! Do you want food?" he asked. The tension inside me fell away and was replaced by not a little relief I had someone to chat to. I thought I wouldn't sleep because I was too watchful, but I hadn't accounted for boredom. Keeping watch with nothing to occupy you when you are already tired just doesn't work.

Later on, I woke with a jolt. I nodded off and then woke myself again with a snore. I couldn't stay awake. What about my wallet, phone and rucksack? If I fell asleep here, they wouldn't be safe. I would have to get in the sleeping bag with my valuables, including my rucksack, shoved in the corner under my head so I'd be disturbed if anyone touched it or searched around me.

So, fitfully, I went through the night. No one did disturb me. I owe a big thank you to Sybille Batten at St Aidan's for the soup and garlic bread, and to whichever member of the church made the cake. I didn't go hungry, at least.

**I'd started to feel vulnerable and question whether I was safe.**

# DAY FOUR

# THE HAVES AND HAVE NOTS

# Day Four: The Haves and Have Nots

So, today is the story of the 'haves and the have nots', or 'me and him'. It rained yesterday and through the night. Not heavy rain, and not all the time, but I have a tent and the rough sleeper, who had heard about what I was doing and who found me, didn't.

It was about 9.30pm when I pitched the tent because the people at Heeley Parish Church had fed both of us and kept us entertained as we talked about homelessness. The ground was wet, and I told my companion that we could share the tent. Did I want to share the tent? No, if I'm honest. He told me he hadn't showered for about a week, so he hadn't changed his clothes for that long either, and he also said that the amount of alcohol he drinks has terrible effects on his bowels.

Not a very attractive prospect! But I was absolutely prepared to share. He said no, though, so I tried to persuade him and in the end he said if it really rained hard he'd use it as shelter. That was that. During the night I heard him snoring and groaning. I heard the rain on the tent too. But he stayed where he was. Deep down, I knew that part of the reason he wouldn't share was that to him, I was the CEO of the organisation he uses, and I couldn't bridge that gap. And it is a massive gap.

At 7am I packed the tent away as he chatted to me from under his wet sleeping bag. As I walked into the city centre I found myself welling up, upset and fighting back the need to cry. Was it because in his life, a wet sleeping bag had become good enough? Maybe. I know I'm struggling to believe that. Or perhaps because I had felt so impotent each time I'd woken up in the night. My need to understand and to make the world just slightly better was wounded by a sense of failure or rejection.

There was another thought swimming around in my head. Earlier in the evening he had described his habit of drinking too much and getting into fights. He isn't a small man, and he reacts to things that make him angry but then, when sober, regrets it. He added something like: "But I can cope with it, if I can cope with what my dad did to me, I can cope with anything." Most people who end up sleeping rough have experienced severe childhood traumas. It's something that creates distance between themselves and the society around them because life becomes an exercise in survival, and trusting others isn't a great survival technique. The outcomes of trauma aren't socially pretty: crime, addiction, aggression and much more. Anything that helps to numb the pain and survive. For some it gets too much, and death seems the best option. I want to shout this story from the rooftops because ending homelessness has to start with understanding this story, just as much – if not more – as with building good quality, affordable homes.

**Was it because in his life, a wet sleeping bag had become good enough?**

## DAY FIVE

# I DON'T WANT TO SEEM UNGRATEFUL, BUT...

# Day Five (A):
# I don't want to seem ungrateful, but...

Last night, after I'd bedded down, a former rough sleeper turned up to see me. Steve lived a five minute drive away from Shiregreen Church. He'd texted me and asked if I wanted coffee or tea (he doesn't touch alcohol) but it wasn't just coffee he brought. He'd made sandwiches, had two bananas and a box of shortbread. 'What's in the sandwiches?" I asked.

"Does it matter. Just get them down ya."

"What's in them?"

Eventually he said, "Bacon, lettuce and tomato."

"I'm veggie," I replied.

"What do you want to be that for, you ungrateful sod?"

I suddenly have very few proper choices. In general, I'm really grateful for food I've had so far but I miss my kitchen and choosing what I'm going to eat. And that's just the tip of the iceberg.

On Tuesday night when I was walking to Heeley, I passed Bramall Lane when the burger vans had opened and carpark stewards were getting in place for the match. It suddenly struck me that even if I wanted to go, as a rough sleeper, it was beyond me. I had virtually no money, I was carrying a rucksack that I'd have to leave somewhere to get in, but more importantly, I didn't feel part of a society that can do those things or be accepted in those places, and that was only on day three.

I went and sat in a park to kill two hours and stewed over a simple and obvious fact; I can walk down the same streets as everybody else, but I can't go to many of the places most others can go. Even in a well-known fast-food place, once I'd ordered, I felt I was being monitored. I took my coffee and walked away instead of sitting inside. The baggage and appearance weigh heavy and, I think, define me when people look at me.

James, another former rough sleeper, phoned me up to ask how it was going. For nearly two decades he lived this transient lifestyle, addicted to illegal drugs, surviving on the street for long periods. "It's more than that mate," he said when I described my observations. "I watched couples holding hands and just walking down the street, going in shops or wherever. I'd have loved that. You watch people go into restaurants and you know they're not places for you." As a rough sleeper, you occupy a different universe.

A little later, James said, "At night when I was carrying my stuff to bed down, I didn't want anyone to see me. I wanted to disappear. If you have a quiet night and there's nothing to write about, treasure it!" Well, last night I had a quiet night!

**I can walk down the same streets as everybody else, but I can't go to many of the places most others can go.**

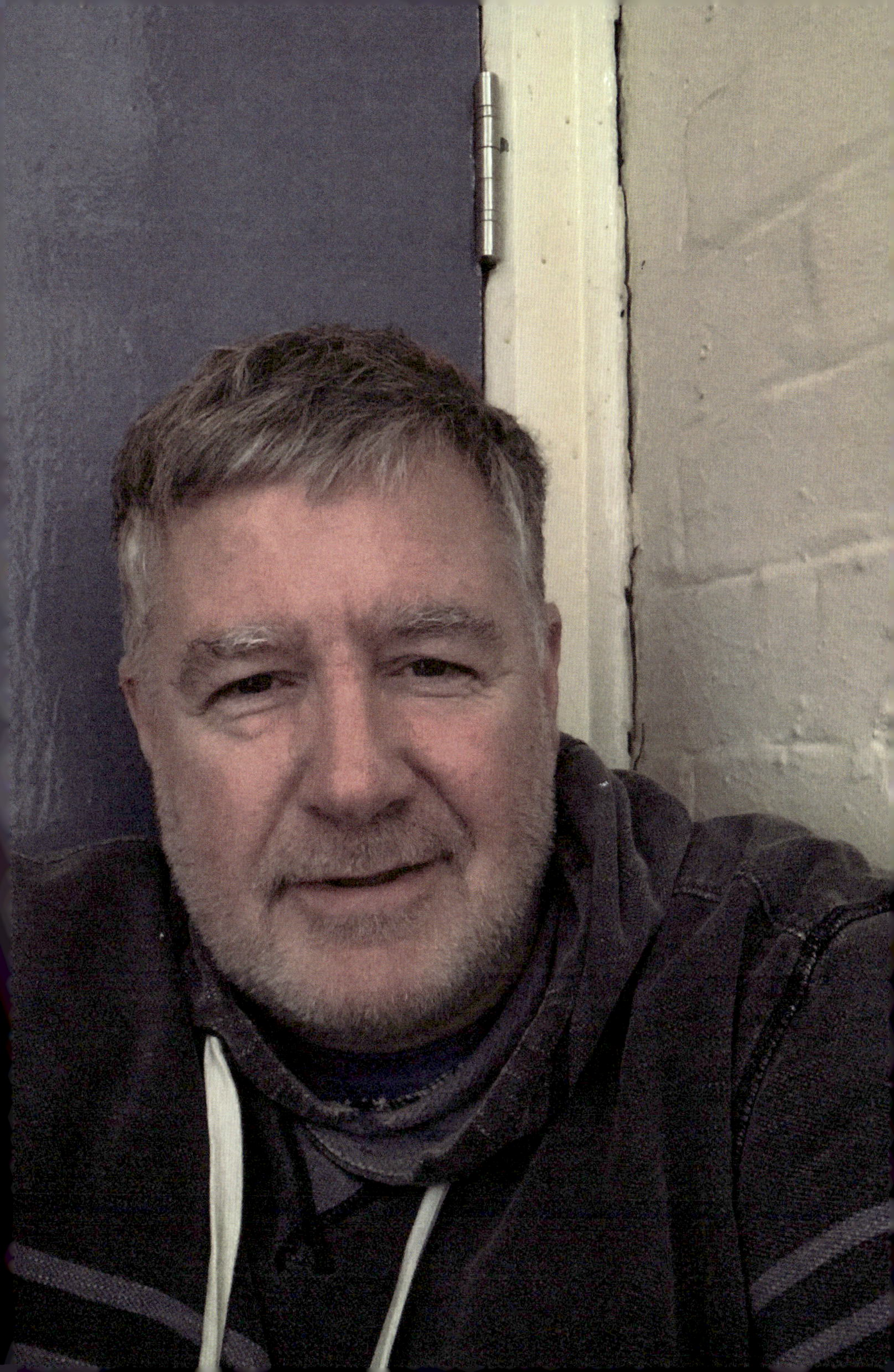

## Day Five (b): 'Tim, you look like s##t."
(How J, another former rough sleeper, greeted me.)

I realised yesterday that I need to change my plans. One of the things I'd wondered about for many years is how difficult it is to function properly if you are sleeping rough, especially if drugs and alcohol are part of the coping strategy.

So far, I've tried to keep up with my work during the day. Yesterday at 11am I realised that all I was good for was reacting. I could answer emails and phone calls and stuff like that but the list of work I want to do and may need to do, that partly lives in my head, had gone. I couldn't think about what to do next without real effort.

We want people who are sleeping rough to be organised enough to make reasonable decisions that will help them in the long run. That means remembering appointments and where those appointments are meant to be. It involves keeping your composure when systems fail, or people don't understand what you're really asking for or trying to say. It involves a lot of things that at my best I can do with ease. But I'm not at my best, and I can't be because I'm not getting enough sleep and I don't feel great about being me and the way some people have looked at me or treated me.

For the remainder of these two weeks, I won't go into the office much. I will write the blog and post it and I will keep the handful of appointments I've got over the next nine days. Otherwise, I will see what I feel like with nothing much between waking and sleeping. A few former rough sleepers have told me that's what I should be doing, so that's what I'll do.

One more thing... today, I had a shower. Thank you, City Taxis! I had an early meeting at their offices and they let me use their shower. It felt so good! Today I took off socks that have been on my feet for four days (I won't give you any more details) because the sad reality is that I haven't wanted to take them off at night, nor my trousers or shirts. I needed them for warmth. I've got clean socks, but there wasn't the option of a clean shirt. Still, it felt good!

**I'm not getting enough sleep and I don't feel great about being me and the way some people have looked at me or treated me.**

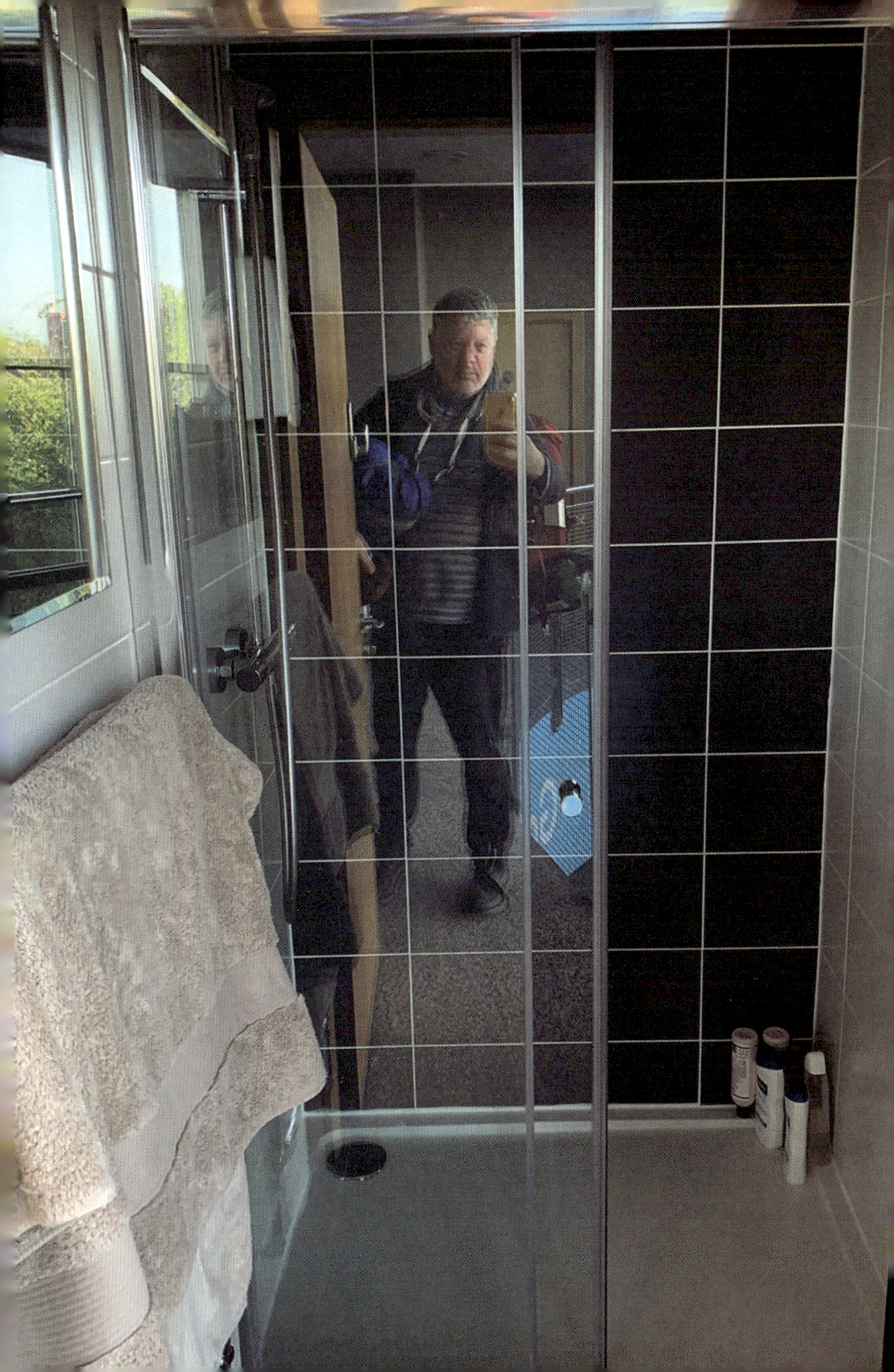

DAY SIX

IT REALLY
IS BEYOND
**BELIEF**

KFC®

# Day Six: It really is beyond belief

I was tired last night, and I had an almost idyllic spot: safe, unseen and clean at Grenoside Parish church. But I didn't sleep. I dozed and kept dozing but that was it, and in the end I just counted down the time until there was no point staying there. I even felt a bit sorry for myself because, to be frank, I wanted to be at home where I could stay in bed with the curtains closed and the door shut. But the truth is that this homelessness of mine is easy compared to the experiences of others and, thankfully, it will remain that way. Just another nine nights for me.

Imagine, though, that when I've finished those nine nights I find that my home, the one I left, is no longer mine. Some people are on the street not because they haven't got a home, but because they can't use the one they have. Chris was one of those people. He was cuckooed. Having been on the street previously, he took pity on someone who said they needed his help and let them stay in his rented flat. But it was a con for a gang to get a foot in the door; Chris explained that "they used my kindness as a weakness to systematically destroy me... How could I be so stupid!" The gang took control until Chris was bullied into submission and left, back on the street but with all the responsibility of paying for the rent and other costs of the flat in his name. "How do you explain it to the council? That you let them in?" he said.

I remember the first cuckooing case I dealt with. Stephen took a few days to tell the whole story. He was ashamed. Admitting he had been bullied and victimised wasn't easy. He felt weak and stupid. Even worse, after putting the story on the table he was left with choices he was afraid of.

Housing services could do nothing until he had reported it as a crime. But that meant naming his abusers and tormentors. He was too afraid of them. They would find him on the street. He was afraid to give the tenancy up because that would mean they would be evicted, and they would blame him. More fear.

All the time he was accruing debts. Everything was in his name. What a mess. What should he do? Chris did report being cuckooed to the police but he was told that because he had invited them in, there was nothing they could do. It would be easy at this point to just blame the system. The big bad system. And there is just cause for that, but we keep reducing the size of the system so it creaks and sometimes fails when it has to deal with less common issues like this. And cuckooing, however you look at it, is complicated. The frontline team of the 'system' cares – I'm part of it – and most of the time we get there, even if sometimes we have to add 'eventually' to that statement.

There's no risk of me being cuckooed, thank God, but if you saw me on the street today you wouldn't know that, would you?

> **He was ashamed. Admitting he had been bullied and victimised wasn't easy. He felt weak and stupid.**

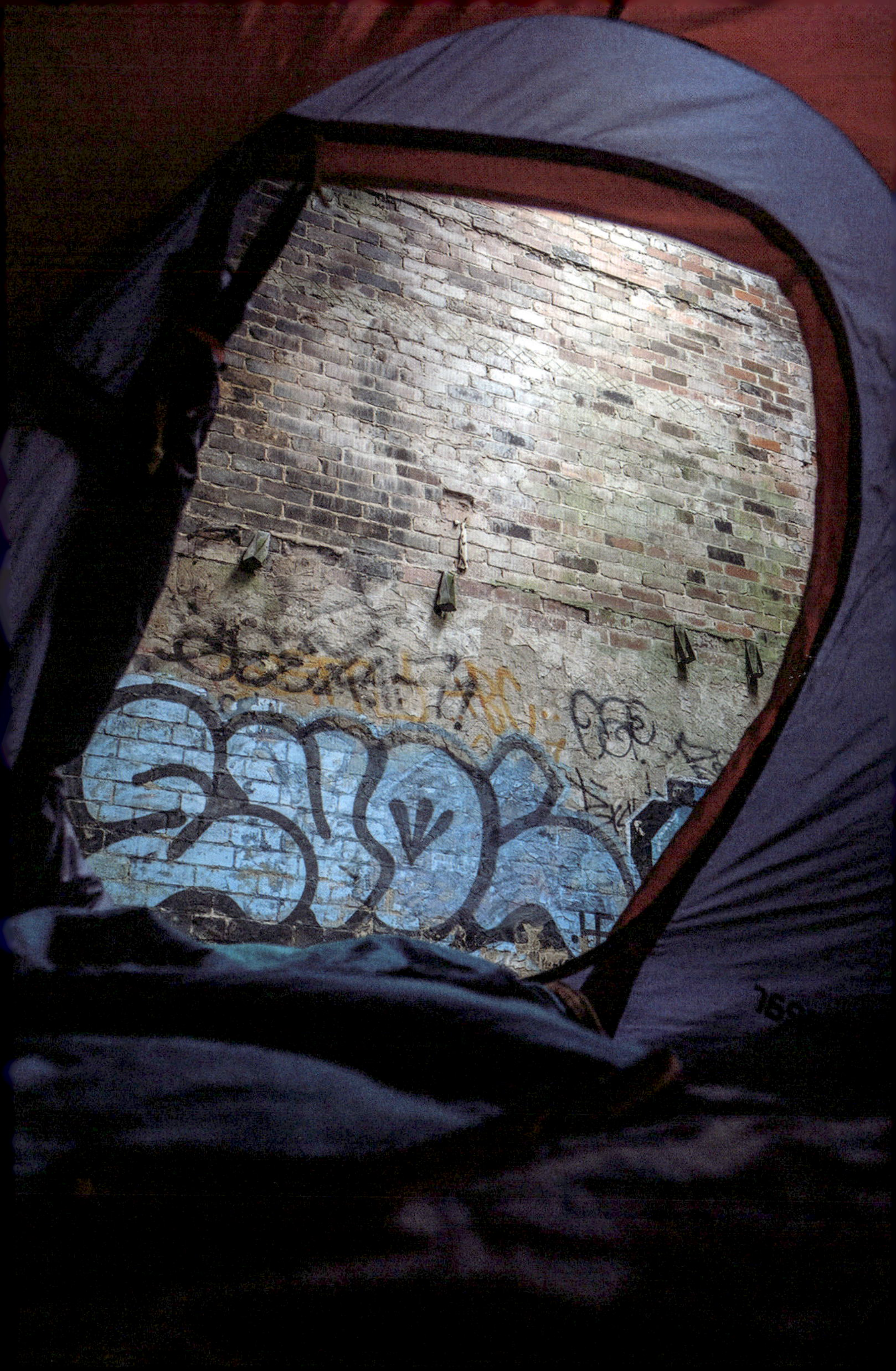

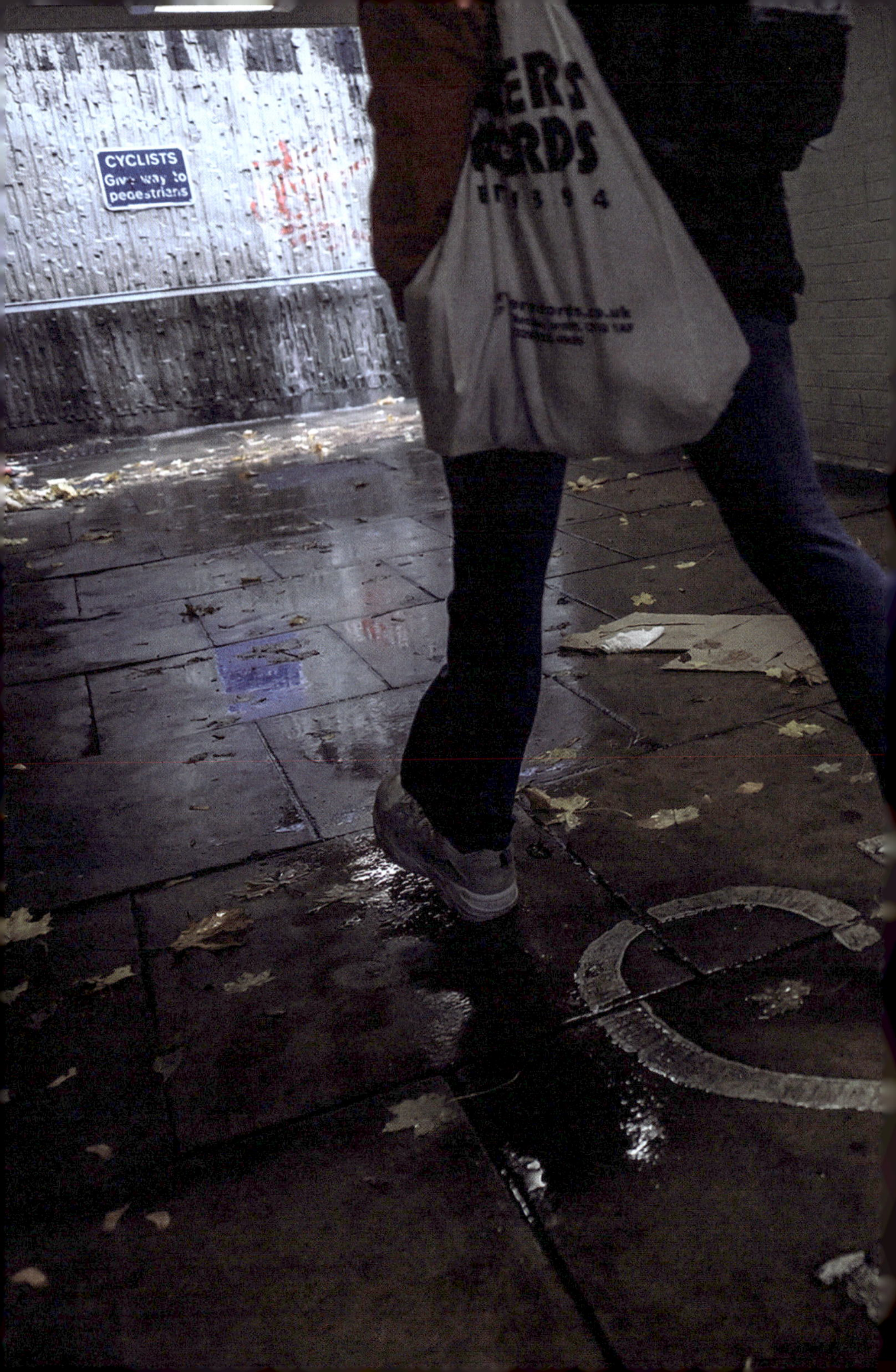
CYCLISTS
Give way to pedestrians

# DAY SEVEN

# RAIN, RAIN, GO AWAY...

## Day Seven: Rain, rain, go away...

I was sat in the Winter Gardens purely and simply because it was dry. I needed to be on my way but the weather was awful, and as I watched a couple dressed for an evening in town – no coats, just shirt sleeves – I felt the first pangs of jealousy because they didn't need to worry about getting wet. I don't know what real rough sleepers do, but uppermost in my mind was keeping dry. It would be cold later and this rain would soak me to the skin. 'Stay dry, stay dry', was the message coming from a deep instinct. 'You can't afford to get ill.' Should I spend money and get the bus? I didn't know. Maybe I'd have to. Decisions, decisions. 'I don't have much money... I'd rather buy a hot drink.'

Suddenly I felt totally dispirited, as if the tedium and pointlessness of being me in that minute and all the hours ahead had been captured in one moment of feeling. I was empty. I didn't know why I was doing this. All around me, people were living. Friends meeting on a work break, a small girl seeming happy and at home in her dad's presence, a woman changing out of her wet cycling over-trousers ready for whatever she was going onto, tourists new to the Winter Gardens. I was waiting, just waiting, and totting up what the cost of what my decision would be. I thought of James' description of watching couples holding hands and knowing that joyfulness wasn't his. Was this one of those moments?

But then the sun came out. Yes! As down as I had felt, now I had to be on it, no time for sentiment. How long would the break last? I got to Dronfield just as the rain started and found a bus shelter to stand in, then I saw a line of dry ground under the overhang in front of the shops nearby. Sod it. People could think what they wanted about me; I was going to sit there, homeless looking, homeless feeling, tired, and I couldn't care less.

45 minutes later, I discovered that St Andrew's Community Church had been open all along and the after-school club were waiting to hear about my journey. A timely reminder it's not actually real for me... but try telling me that at the time.

> ... I felt the first pangs of jealousy because they didn't need to worry about getting wet.

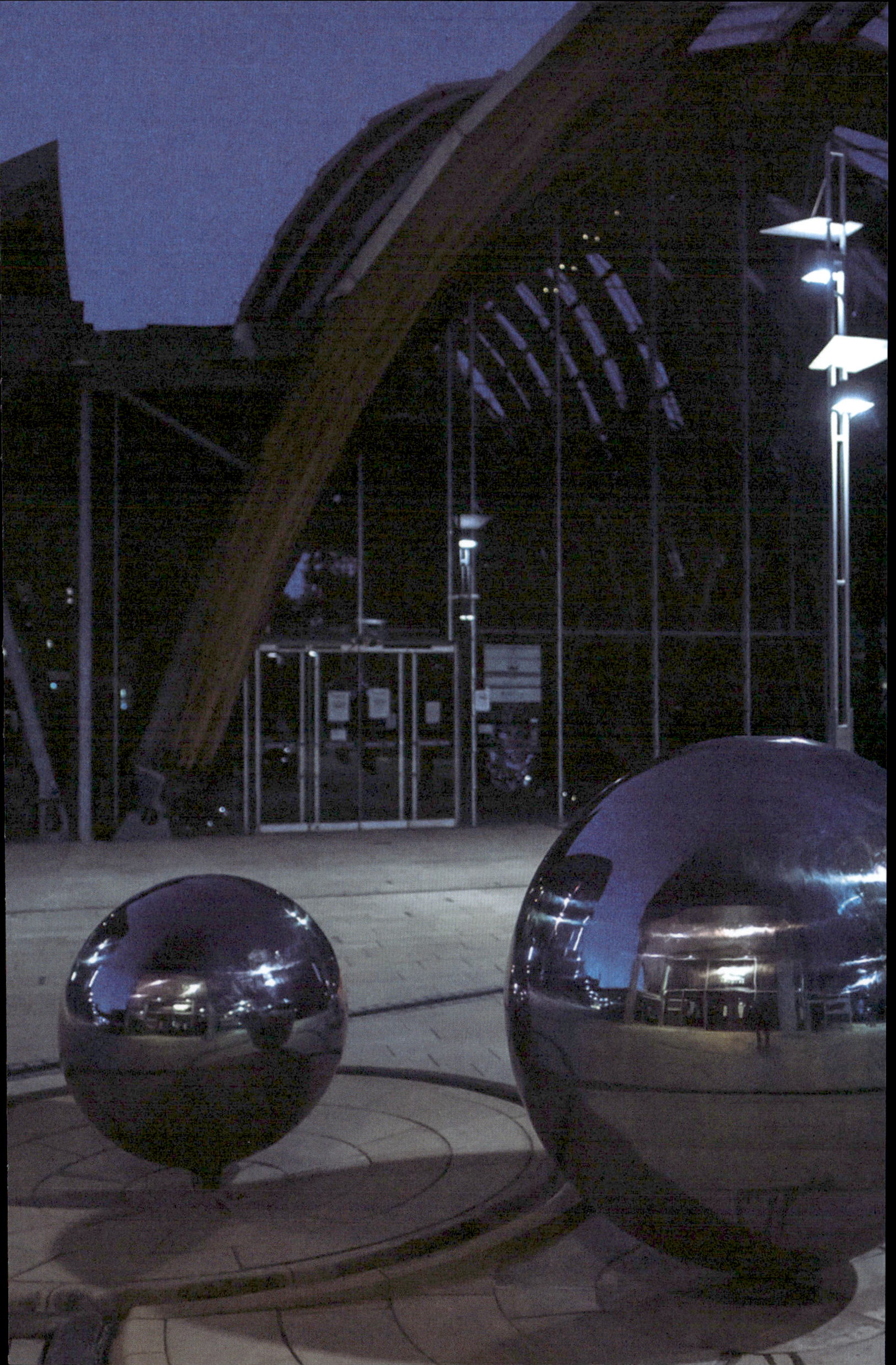

# DAY EIGHT

# AND
## STILL IT
## GOES ON

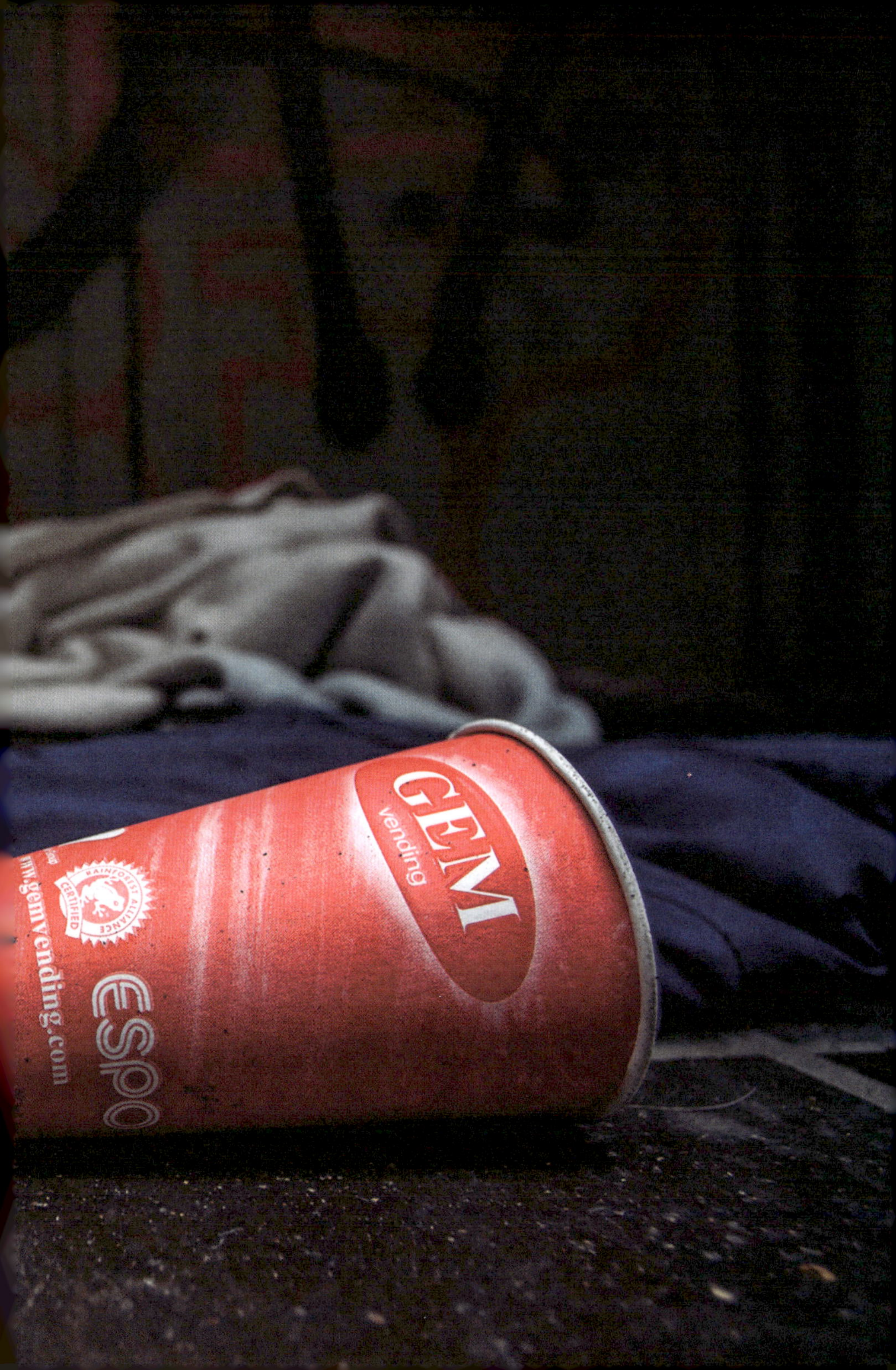
GEM
vending
gemvending.com

# Day Eight: And still it goes on...

What a beautiful day! The sun shone and I walked. For quite a while there was nothing about the day that had anything to do with homelessness. I was just a walker in the countryside. No one would guess otherwise. All would have been well, apart from the fact that I'm trying to stick to some guidelines learned from real rough sleepers which meant that the lovely country pub was off limits.

I was once in Sheffield City Centre with a lad who was one or two steps away from street homelessness. We were next to Café Rouge, and I asked him if he wanted a coffee. "In there? No way." He looked at me as if I was joking with him. To me it was a coffee shop. To him, it was another world, a place he was excluded from. A self-exclusion. He looked around as we went in, as if he expected some bouncer to step in front of him. Within ten minutes the myth had been busted. It was just another place to get a coffee.

The country pub was in my self-exclusion zone. So what? Well, my phone battery was dead and I wanted to charge it. I could have done that in the pub. There would be somewhere else, surely? But there wasn't. At my destination there wasn't anywhere. So, no phone. Also, no conversation. I sat and watched people pass by with an occasional 'Hi'. I sat in one place and then moved to another and found a bench. I sat there for a while and then moved somewhere else. Killing time that didn't want to die. No conversation. No cup of tea or coffee. People passing by doing simple things. Walking the dog. Popping into the Co-op. Overhearing bits of others' conversations, friends processing thoughts as they walked and talked. I felt alone. I was alone, without even a phone to check.

At 6pm I met Gary the vicar who had food for me and a socket to plug in the phone. I talked too much. I could hear myself doing it. It was wonderful. The phone came alive. Messages. I hadn't checked in with my friends and family (which is one of the conditions of me doing this; I'm the only rough sleeper with a 'risk assessment' that requires certain actions on my part). Then the full weight of loneliness descended. Not mine: the loneliness of others who weren't getting messages, who didn't have people checking in with them, who weren't ever asked if they were safe. As the full weight of that loneliness dawned, I just started to sob. And I sobbed and sobbed.

I know that most homeless people have other homeless people, but it's not the same. I know it's not because each Christmas we hear the same thing: "I bloody hate Christmas!" Why? Because it's their big annual reminder of not having those messages of love and care.

**To me it was a coffee shop. To him, it was another world, a place he was excluded from. A self-exclusion.**

EORGE STREET

SHARING BAG

PLZ HELP A
GIVE A LiT
CHAM

# DAY NINE

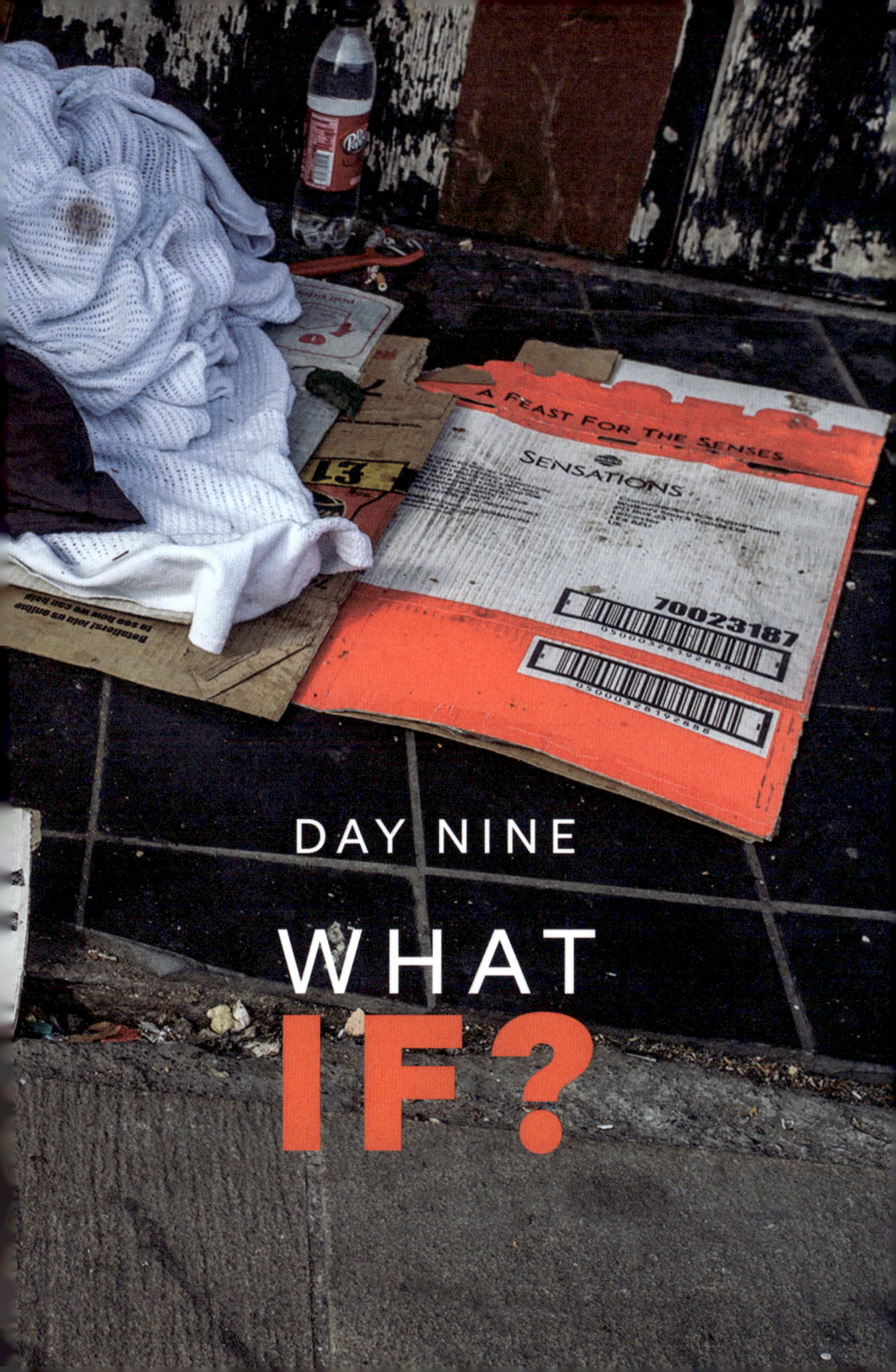

# WHAT IF?

# Day Nine: What If?

Today's blog was going to be about Richard. This journey was supposed to be his. He thought of it and wanted to do it. I'm doing it as a replacement; I didn't start 2022 with any idea that I would spend 14 nights with no home.

But first I need to tell you about my body. For the last few days, it has objected loudly, shouting 'this is no way to treat me!' at the top of its voice. When I get up, I've got a picture in my mind of my dad in his seventies, slowly stretching when he stood up, as if he was putting some of his bones back in place, a place they were tired of being. That's me this morning. I wake two or three times every night to reposition myself in the least uncomfortable shape. Usually, I move from sleeping on one side to the other and then to sleeping on my back. I don't think I ever sleep on my back at home.

I am tired. But I have to get up and leave. Years of listening to people tells me that the time I need to leave depends on the place I've found to sleep. One man was accepted sleeping in an old hut near some factories and would sometimes stay all day, mentally unwell and avoiding human contact. But that is rare, I think. Most get up and leave before daytime users come and see them. They don't want to lose a good spot. Typically, I would have no choice. Aching bones and an unwilling body would stand for nothing. Trudge, trudge, trudge. Off I go into another day which holds little promise.

So, back to Richard. Aston Church was the first place he ever slept rough. It was the day his bridge with home was finally burnt. I have all sorts of 'what if?' questions that imagine early interventions which would stop his years of street life, of drug dependency, begging, being the victim of two serious assaults on the street, being taken off the street into hospital. Not to mention developing the nasty side of his character to defend himself. Years and years and years of lost talent, lost life, lost relationships.

But the truth is, my 'what ifs' were needed sooner. What if his mum hadn't died? What if his dad had coped better with her death? What if the wider family hadn't threatened his dad's ability to cope with two young children? What if... what if... what if?

Recently, Richard asked me what it was like to grieve. He didn't think he'd ever done it. Not for his mum, because he thought he might be to blame. What could a small child have done? But he was cuddling her when her heart stopped. The thought that he should have done something has stayed with him. He didn't grieve for his dad. He had rebelled against his dad. His dad never gave up on him and Richard knew it. When he died, Richard used more heroin. It took him to a happier place, away from grief.

And now? Well, Richard is getting there. He has a life. Why did it have to take so long?

> **But first I need to tell you about my body. For the last few days, it has objected loudly, shouting 'this is no way to treat me!' at the top of its voice.**

Sheffi
Heart o
the City
info@heartofcity2.co
0800 731 5515
@Sheff_HoC2
sheffieldhoc2
www.heartofcity2.co

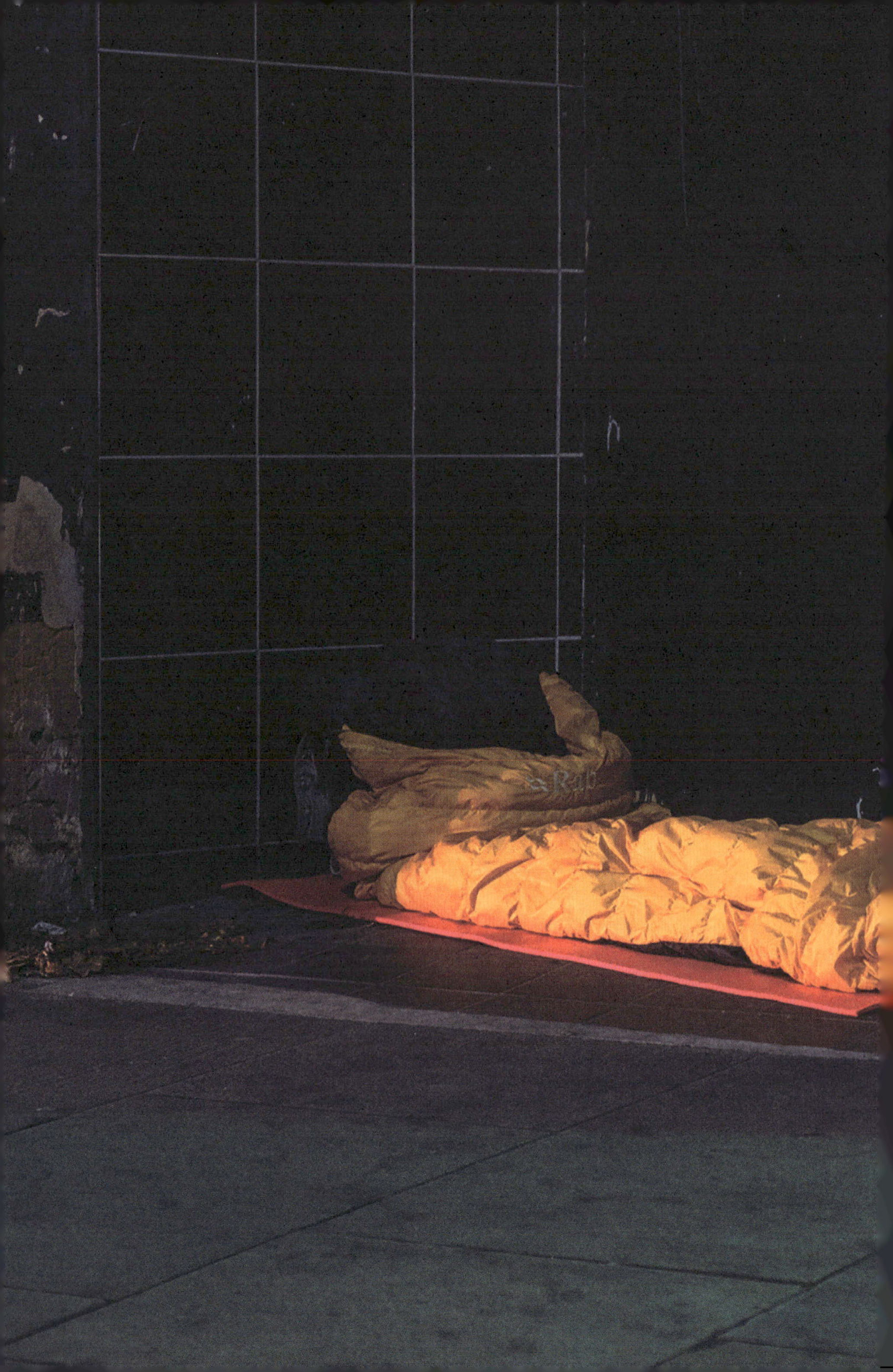

DAY TEN

# I WANT TO BE WHERE YOU ARE

## Day Ten: I want to be where you are

**5.30pm.** It's cold. I imagine the cars on the road are warm inside. I'm thinking about that because I'm sat outdoors, shivering. I've found a bit of shelter, an L-shaped wall, which stops the wind. Shortly, I'll get up and walk about because my bum is cold; the paving slab beneath me is drawing out warmth. But I've been walking for a while, and I need to sit for a bit. Maybe I should get my sleeping bag and mattress out, but it feels too early. I can smell Chinese food. The aroma is tempting but I can't afford it. The church I'm at will feed me, which reminds me that I'm not really homeless.

**5.45pm.** My bum and the slab feel the same temperature. Maybe I should stay. But what will I do? I wonder where the cars are heading. I'm jealous of them. I imagine warm rooms, kettles boiling, the TV on, paused for a conversation about the day. But it's all somewhere else and I'm here. If I do get up and move from here, where do I go? What do I do? A couple of lads are walking past me and swearing at each other. Just for a moment I stop thinking about the cold and hope they walk by and ignore me. They do. If I were walking into my home now, I'd head straight for the shower and stand in it to let the water warm me. Then I'd check the treat drawer; maybe there'd be some fruit loaf I could toast and melt butter on. Dreams. Dreams. All I have is thoughts of being elsewhere. I'm tired. I could go home but if this were real, I wouldn't even have that thought.

The wall isn't stopping the draught as much as I'd like. It's 5.55pm and, fortunately, someone has arrived at the church. I have a chance to go into the warmth before I come back out to sleep. I'm not really homeless.

**6.30am.** It was cold last night, and I have a really good sleeping bag. How did others cope? It's only October! The thing that strikes me as I get up is that I smell. My feet stink. They override the other odours until I put my boots on. Then I can smell my clothes. It's my tenth day and if I'd been kicked out of home, I might not have found places like The Archer Project. And even if I had, I'm not sure how I would feel about admitting I smell.

**8.30am.** I got a lift into Sheffield and am sat in the train station. I can't describe how different I feel from the people around me. They are busy, clean, dressed for the business of the day ahead. They are purposeful. All I can think of is that I smell. I didn't know why it was important to have just one set of clothes when I set off ten days ago. I do now. I am dehumanised in a way I couldn't have imagined. I am, somehow, less than the people I meet or see. I am ashamed of how I am. The danger is that with time I will forget, and this will become my new normal.

> **All I have is thoughts of being elsewhere. I'm tired. I could go home but if this were real, I wouldn't even have that thought.**

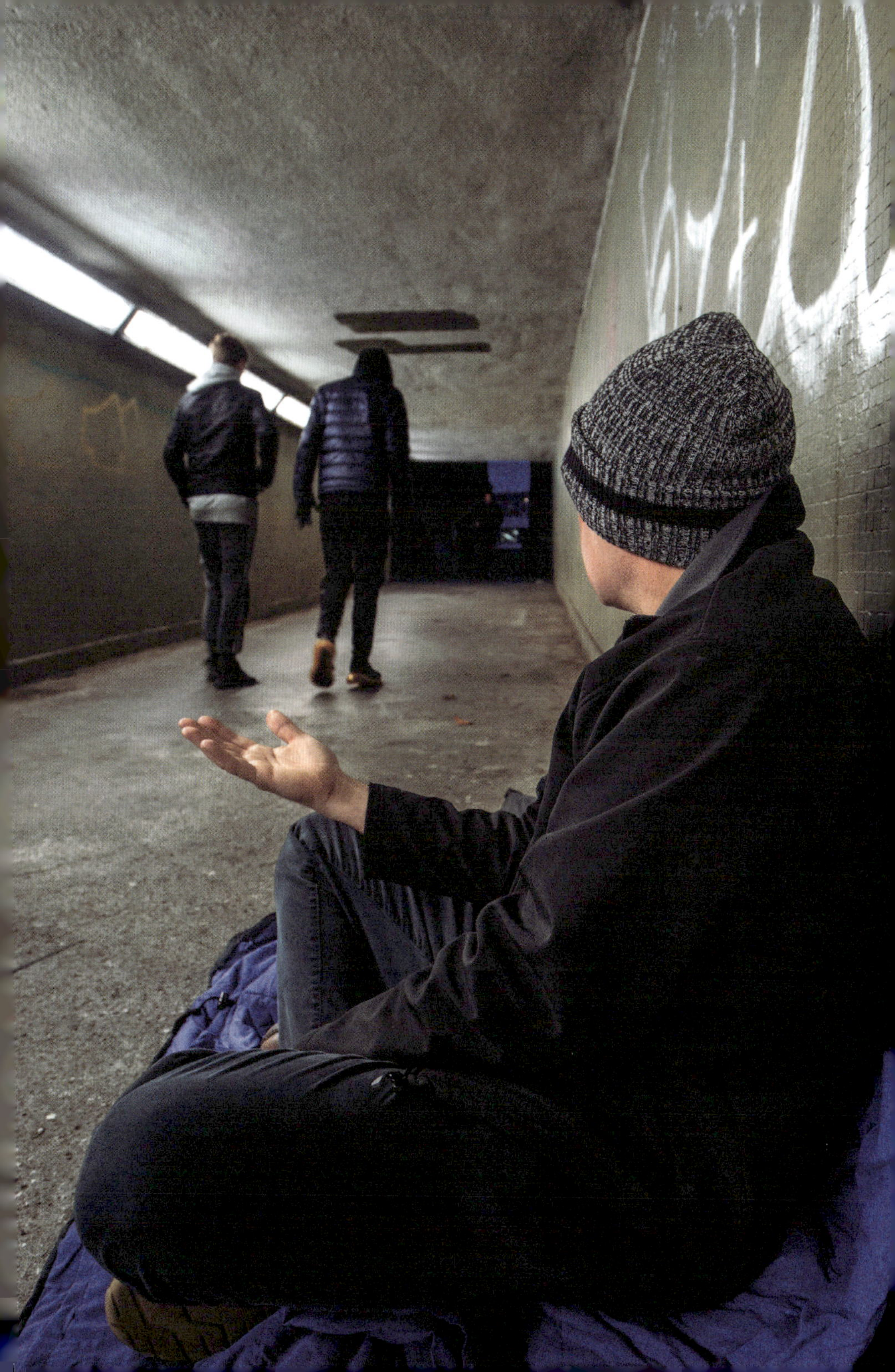

# DAY ELEVEN

## LEST WE FORGET

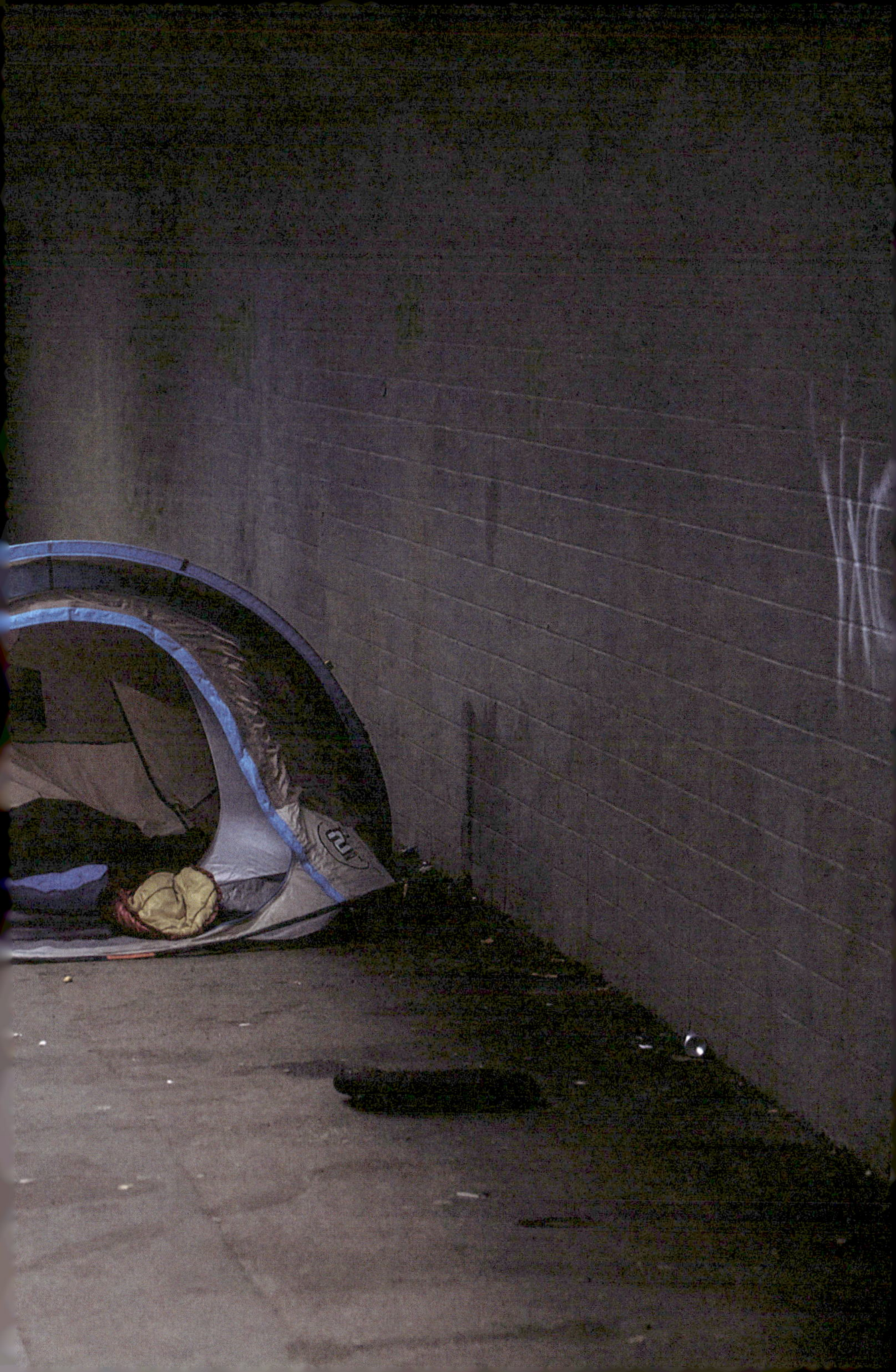

# Day Eleven: Lest We Forget

It's 5.52am and I've had a fairly good sleep. Lying here in the beautiful doorway of St Mary's Church, Ecclesfield, a cloudy moon is alone in the sky. When I went to sleep the sky was full of stars. I don't know their names.

If Gav was here, he might tell me something about constellations. He died in 2020 after years of alcohol abuse. When I first knew him, sometimes passed out on the grass outside Sheffield Cathedral, I couldn't have guessed at the intelligence that filled his head. I wouldn't have guessed the horrors either. The violent death he witnessed, the rejection by his stepdad, the journey into the care system which didn't work for him, the loss of a daughter, and so the story goes on.

This doorway is poignant too. The last time I was here was for the funeral of K. 20 years of military service, three stripes on his arm and enough trauma to sink a battleship. He used The Archer Project for just a few months. In that time, we saw the two sides of K: a joy and zest for life and the tremendous weight of internal pain that he couldn't shed. He let it go in the only way he knew.

This may sound strange, but I've just sat and named a whole list of people who used our project and others in Sheffield, who are now dead. And yet it doesn't feel morbid. Sat here, it feels respectful. Jason, Liam, Spence, Jo, John, Stephen, Charlotte… you don't need to hear all the names and it's far too long a word count for a blog. Besides, there are too many for me to remember and if I feel any sadness this morning it's because I think they shouldn't be forgotten.

But I don't feel sad, I feel hopeful. I set out on this journey to have a conversation about homelessness and the response has been amazing. That can only be a good and hopeful thing. You've got to have hope, haven't you? And I slept well last night. I think that makes a difference too.

I've got a can of beer here and that reminds me of someone. He used to open his bottle of drink first thing in the morning. It was the very first thing he did to get him going when he lived in a tent. He had been a cook and we agreed with him that if he could come into the centre without that early morning drink, he could help in the kitchen. At first, he lasted till 8am before leaving for his drink. After a little while it was 8.30, then 9. He had hope and he worked at it with just a little help from us. When he died it was in his own home. He hadn't conquered his demons, but he had done enough to be proud. We didn't know about his trauma back then. I wonder what difference that might have made to the journey we offered him?

I have never started the day with alcohol, but maybe today… I think I'll save it for tonight.

> **… I couldn't have guessed at the intelligence that filled his head. I wouldn't have guessed the horrors either.**

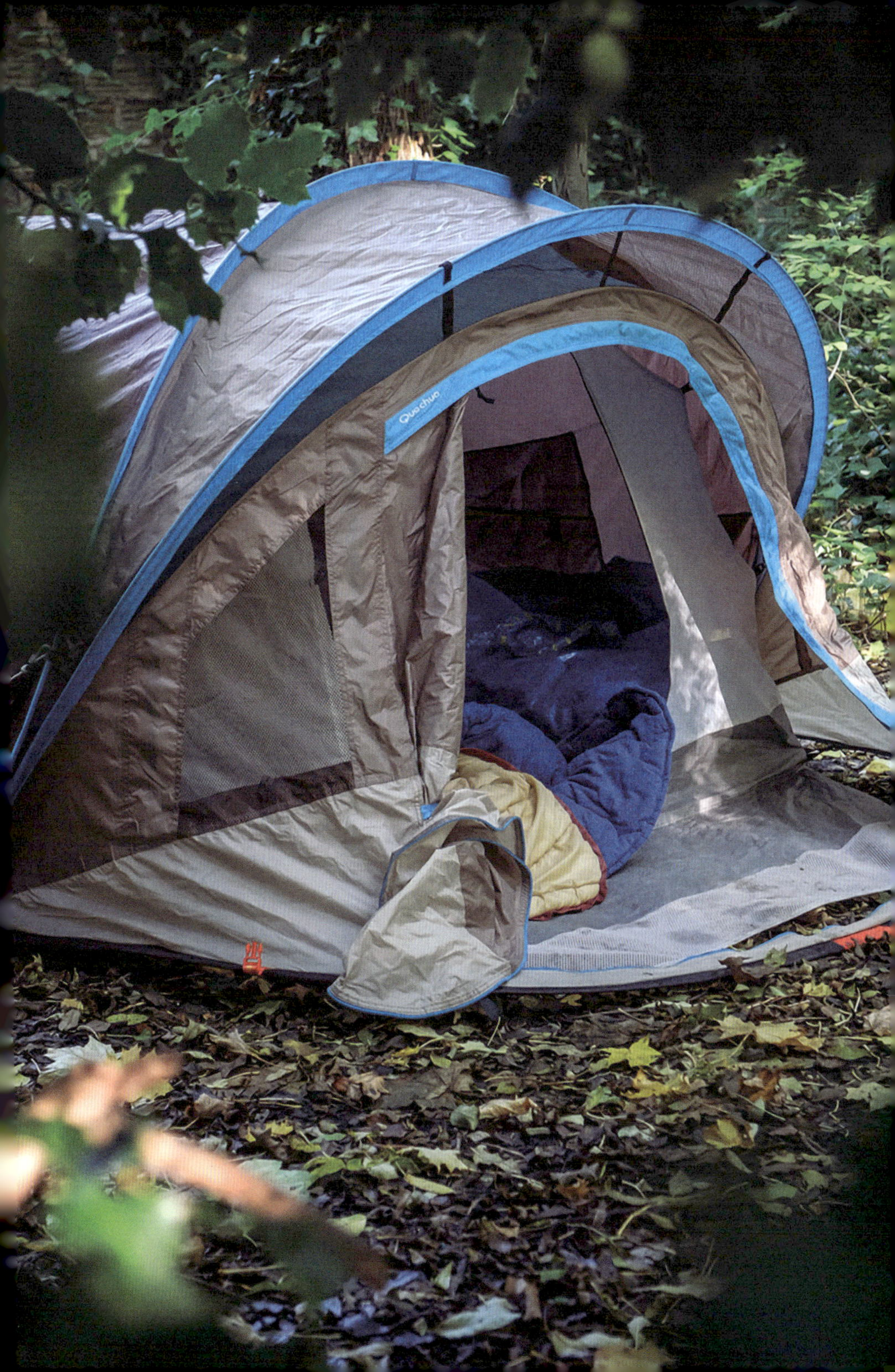
Quechua

# DAY TWELVE

# IT'S
### EVERYWHERE

THE BIBLE

HIGHER

NLT

# Day Twelve: It's Everywhere

I'm in Eyam, famously known as the Plague Village. I'm not here because it's overrun with homelessness. Though rural homelessness is real, and the locals can tell you about supporting people who have made the countryside their non-home.

Quite simply, Eyam Parish Church is where the idea of a 14-night sleepout began. My day here has felt like a 'break' from being homeless and I feel a bit guilty for not being more hardcore. On my way here I had a conversation with someone who had slept rough for two weeks. It wasn't in a rural village, but it was in her local community. She didn't run away to the city. But most of her homelessness wasn't sleeping rough. She survived by using friends' homes when life went wrong. For her it was always domestic violence. Interestingly, she distinguished between times when there was no physical violence, it was just that home had become dangerous, and real violence when she had to flee for fear of physical injury.

Her two weeks of rough sleeping had been carefully managed. She tried to give the appearance of not being homeless. She visited friends during the day, saying nothing about not being able to go home. Why? Because she was ashamed. She was embarrassed. She thought everybody would think her weak or stupid. So, she acted. She pretended all was okay and spent her time visiting friends. Then, when she had outstayed her welcome, she went to another friend until she felt her only choice was to go and hide in the local churchyard. The next day she would do the same. The churchyard was where she slept.

That was the first time. Then the violence became 'real'. She told her friends and they let her stay for the periods she couldn't go home. She wasn't sleeping rough, but she was homeless. She still felt ashamed. And let's be frank, it was still hardcore homelessness.

Another woman we worked with said that after a while of staying with a friend she felt the need to return to the street. Her friend didn't kick her out. She just felt uncomfortable putting on them. "They were a couple. How could they be a couple with me sleeping on their sofa?" It limited them, she argued. She felt like an intruder and went back to the street.

I felt just a tiny bit of that yesterday as I was welcomed by Merlyn and Paul, who have been supporters of The Archer Project for years. I hadn't been in a home for ten days and felt reluctant to go inside because I smell. I didn't want to take my shoes off as I went in because my feet stink. They didn't make me feel uncomfortable, quite the opposite; being homeless does that for me.

> **She visited friends during the day, saying nothing about not being able to go home. Why? Because she was ashamed.**

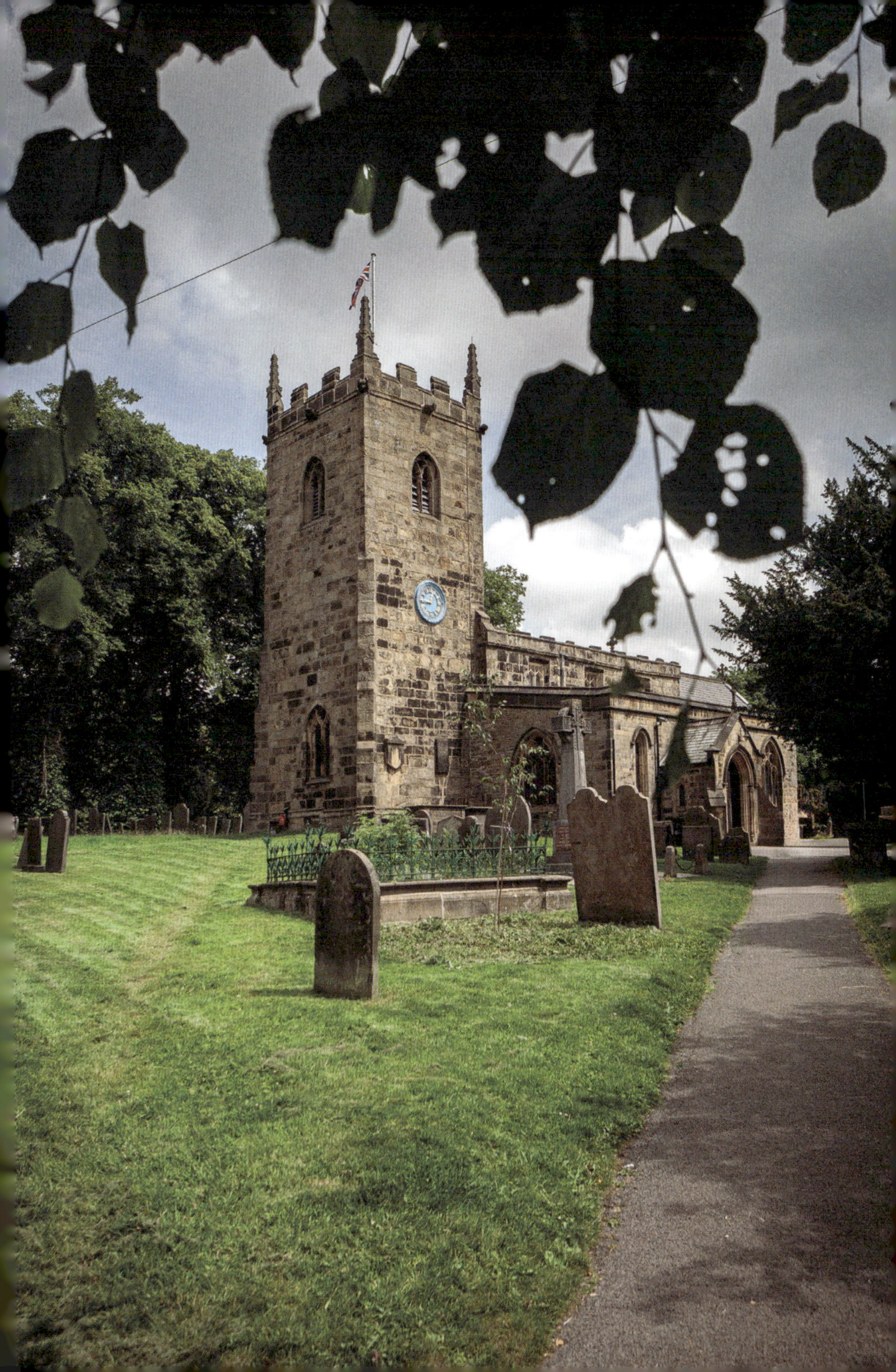

# DAY THIRTEEN

# FIRST SURVIVE, THEN THRIVE.

TRUELOVES GUTTER

# Day Thirteen: First survive, then thrive

I'm sat on The Moor, one of the main shopping streets in Sheffield. It's 8.30am. Shops are getting ready to open and a few familiar faces have walked past me. Two are men who are part of the street homeless population. One has accommodation. He walked past with a can of alcohol in his hand, open. It would be easy for me to judge him; after all he could be at home instead of here and he's drinking early in the morning. I feel conflicted because I know there's a reason he turned to drink. I also know he won't be easy to deal with later in the day if he drinks too much.

I have a day of nothingness ahead. It is beyond boredom. It is surviving, with no other purpose than to get through the day. There are moments of relief, and for some that comes in the form of alcohol or drugs. Yesterday, for me, it was Carla. She spotted me and waved. I came alive. A smiling face I knew was walking towards me!

Carla has never been homeless, but her dad was. Homeless and a street alcoholic, he was killed on Fargate. He wasn't dissimilar to the person who passed me a few minutes ago, except that for Carla's dad, there was a successful career and family life before the series of events came along that led to his breakdown. He hadn't decided to be homeless. He didn't set out to be rejected and judged. When I knew him, he argued powerfully and persuasively, even cantankerously. He was clever. He cared for others on the street. I called him 'The Doctor' because he knew more about health and social care than me. His experience of breakdown and street life left him with little hope. He focused on survival, both his and those he shared his life with. Getting alcohol was part of that. Survival is a different mindset than choice.

All these years later, Carla fights for people whom others continue to judge. It is personal. People who suffer homelessness should have better food, they should have health care, they should have everything that makes life bearable, and it should happen today, now. Now is the most important time. Carla can't change what happened to her dad, but we can change the future for others.

On that note, something else from yesterday. Theresa, responding to my blog and the comments that came from it, talked about the pain of being a mother watching her daughter suffer. Then she thanked The Archer Project and Printed By Us. It reminded me that all this very necessary talk about homelessness isn't complete without the knowledge that people survive and go on to thrive. Something to celebrate!

Find out more about how we employ people with a history of homelessness and take a look at our premium quality, sustainably produced, screen-printed artwork and garments by scanning the QR Code below.

OYDS BANK
CREATED LIKE NO OTHER.
GUINNESS
MADE OF MORE
JCDecaux
HOLLAND &

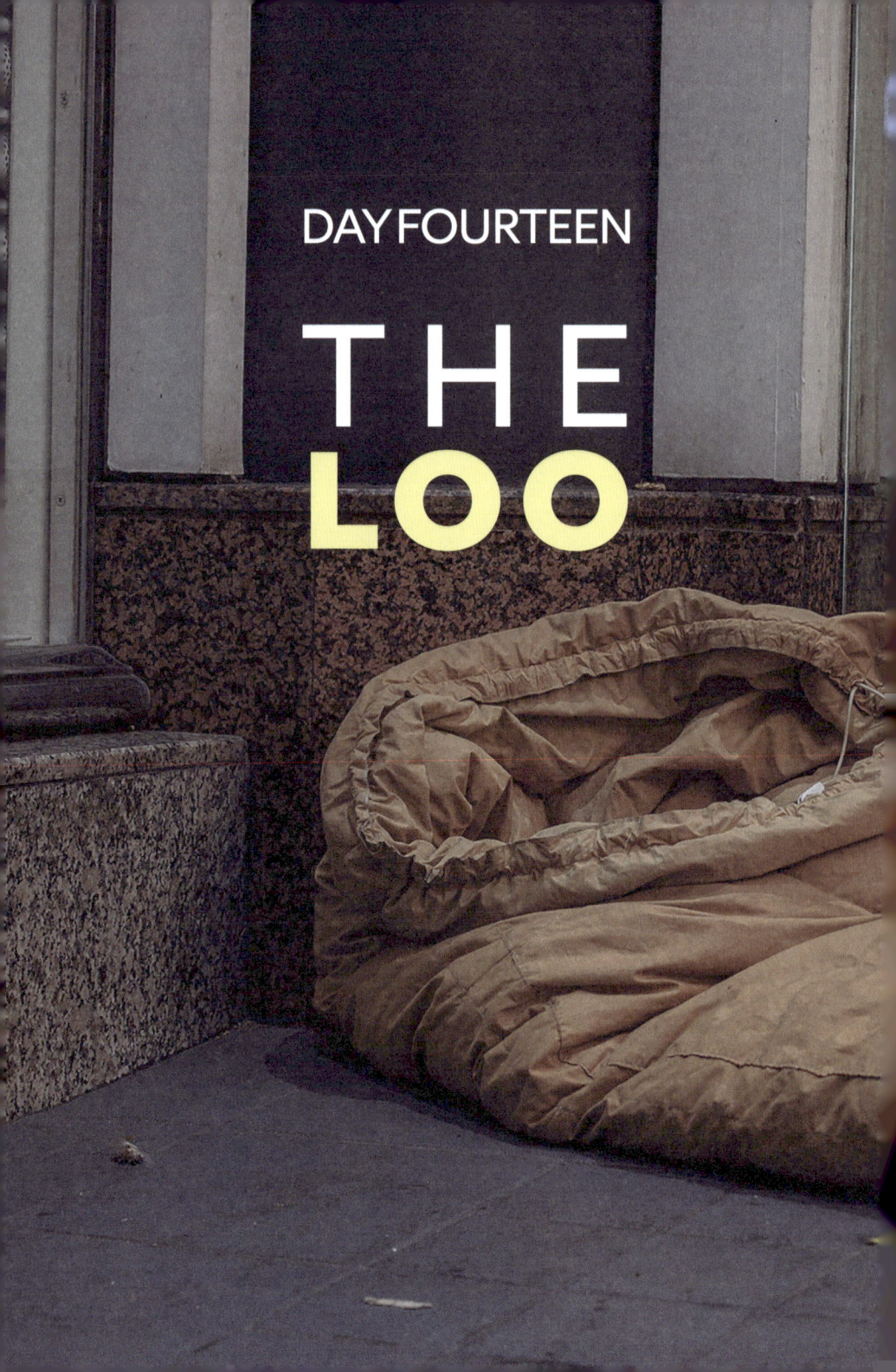

# DAY FOURTEEN
# THE LOO

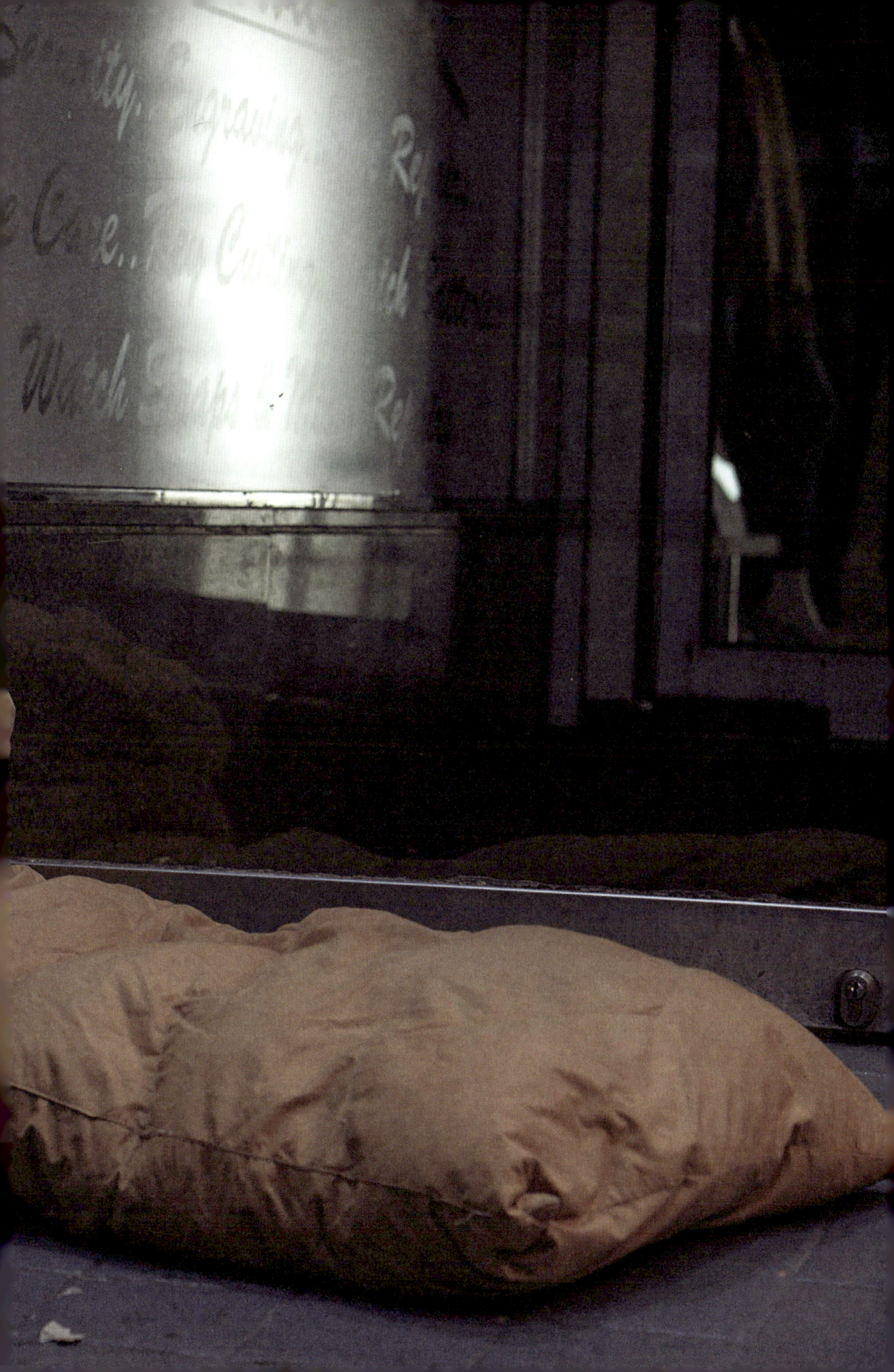

# Day Fourteen: The Loo

One of the most frequent questions I've been asked is, 'What are you doing about the toilet?" Remember, I am not homeless. I have had 14 churchyards to sleep in. Most have given me access to a toilet, though I have had some nights with no loo in sight. Toilets are a problem.

Walking from the car park to The Archer Project's centre at Sheffield Cathedral one morning, I saw Patrick stood gloved up, bag in one hand, shovel in the other and a bucket of soapy water on the ground.

"Just dealing with a pile."

"Oh, that's unpleasant."

"I know, fancy needing to go and there being nowhere!" His sympathy was with the leaver of the deposit. Mine was with him.

I went into this temporary homelessness knowing I have occasional problems with IBS (irritable bowel syndrome). There are moments when my body gives me little warning of the need to go. Sometimes it's an immediate demand. At other times, I can manage about 15 minutes of concentrated effort to get me to a loo. I've been lucky. IBS has only bothered me twice on this sleepout, both times within range of an accessible toilet… accessible to me. But most rough sleepers don't have the access I've had.

One of my rules for the last two weeks has been that I wouldn't go into places to eat or drink that I believe people who are homeless wouldn't use. Needing the toilet made me really question that decision. If you are desperate, surely you take a risk. I remember being in a high street coffee shop chain and seeing someone who was a known street drinker come in and make his way to the toilet. He carried all the traits of someone who lives on the street, and I looked around to see the response of those he passed. They all looked at him, and he stared defiantly back. He knew he was out of place. He looked uncomfortable, but he needed the loo. Since that time many shops and cafés have fitted code locks so that toilets are for customers only. City centre public toilets have closed.

When I was thinking about this blog post, I mentioned to a couple of people that I have a 57 year old bladder, generally in good condition but with a faulty stop/start function. A much younger woman responded, "I've got a 'three baby bladder' and that's useless." She had survived homelessness. I realise toileting and health are individual issues, but they impact each other too. Someone else mentioned being coeliac. It was only when they were diagnosed that they realised how unwell they had felt for years, with an impact on their bowels.

Over these 14 days I've shared much of what I think is hidden about homelessness. We don't wear badges telling people our histories. Our health needs are largely invisible. Maybe this is the most important thing to take away. That invisibility allows us to overlook important things and make unwarranted assumptions. It's probably the worst part about being homeless.

**One of the most frequent questions I've been asked is, 'What are you doing about the toilet?"**

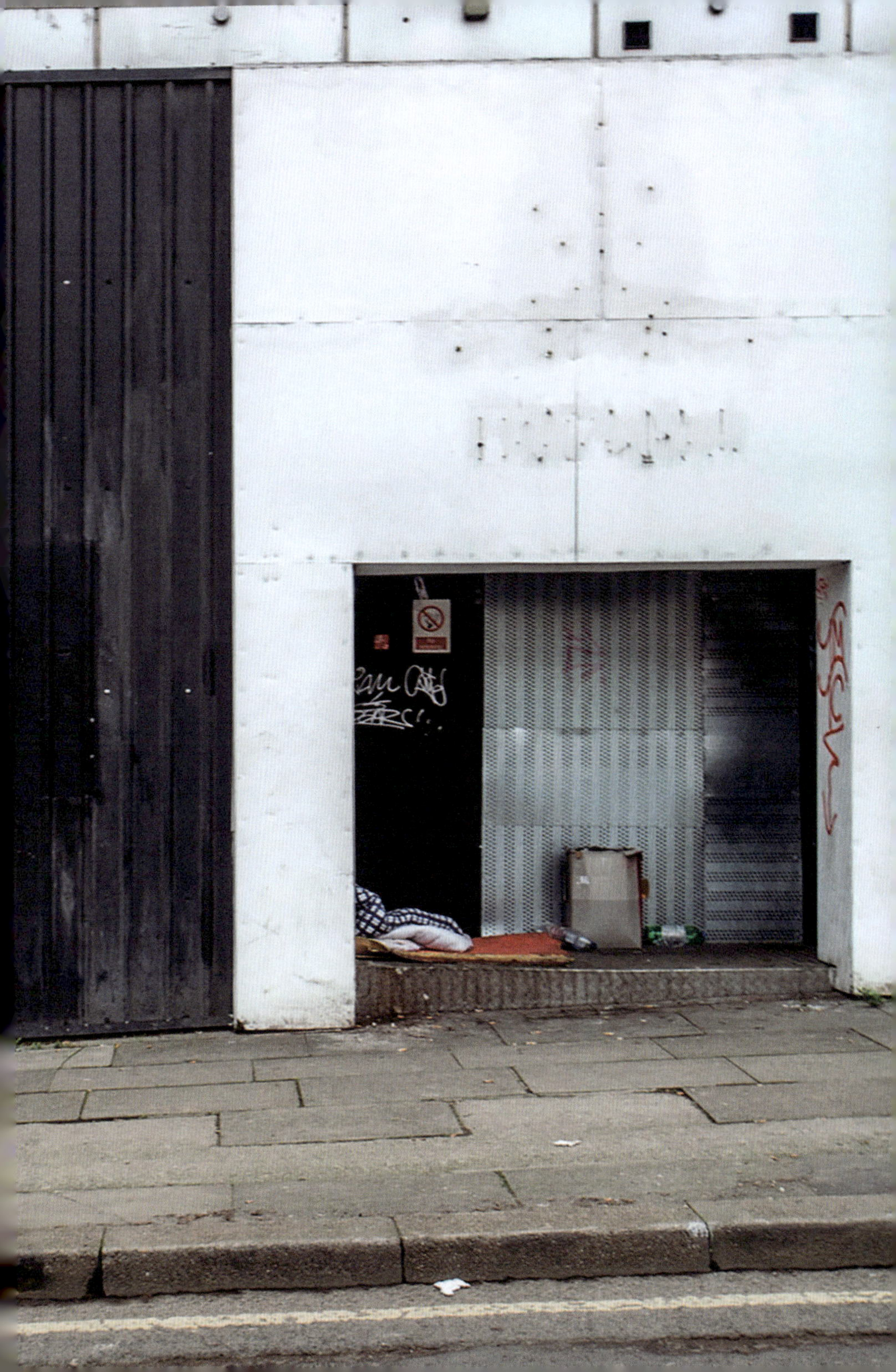

## DAY FIFTEEN

# HAS IT ENDED YET?

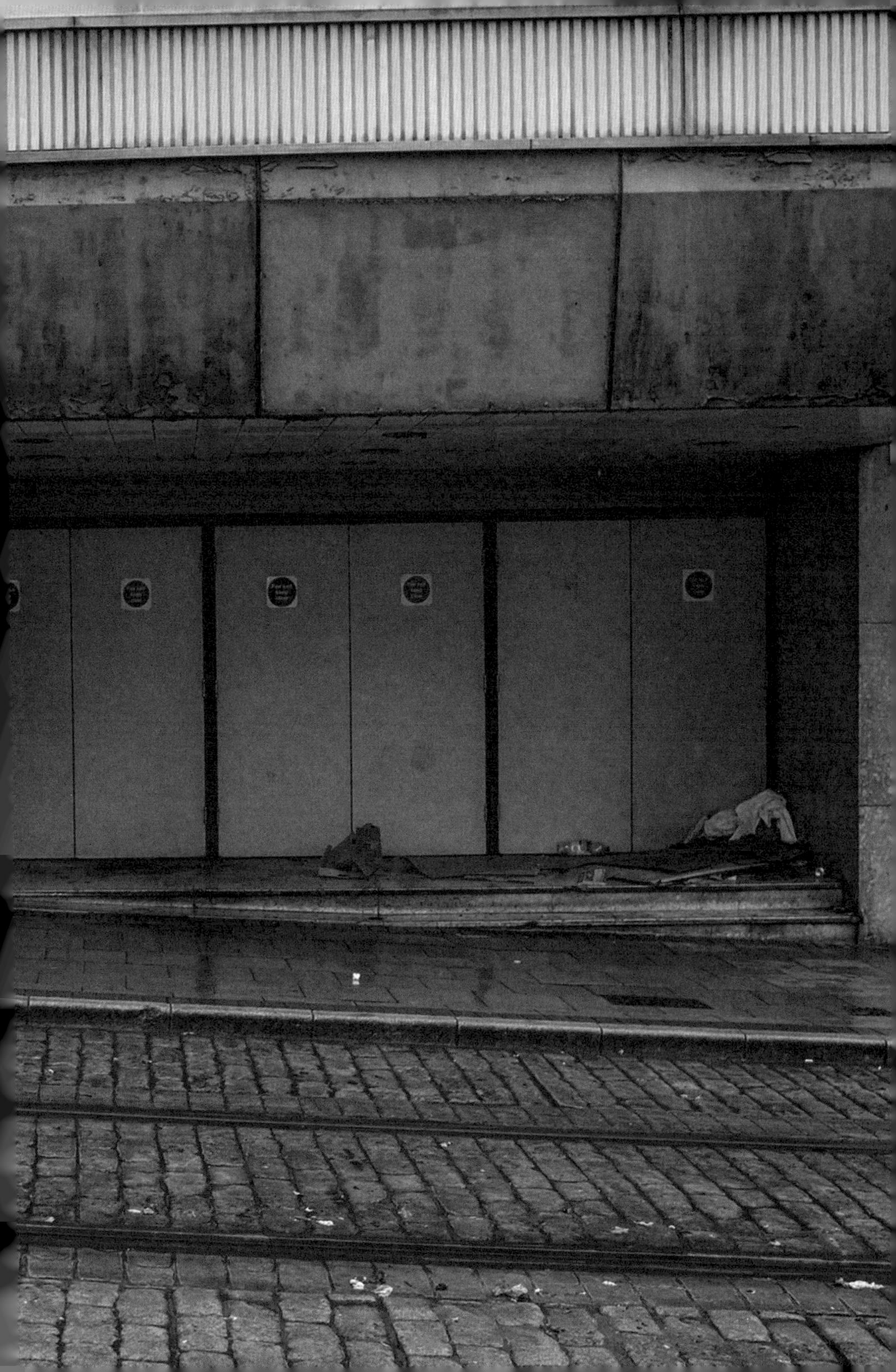

# Day Fifteen: Has it ended yet?

I was awake at just before 6am this morning, lying in my sleeping bag, looking out at a clear sky from the doorway at St John's, Ranmoor. I tucked my shoulders into the bag because it was cold. Today I can go home but instead of elation, I feel drained and empty.

I have no sense of achievement or satisfaction. I realised that if this was the last day of an adventure, walking the Pennine Way or something like that, I would perhaps be feeling sad that it was over but I'd be taking away a trophy of some kind, an objective completed and enjoyed. I haven't enjoyed the last fortnight. I've loved meeting wonderful people and I've made some new friends. But homelessness got into my head and body and that's a horrible experience.

The other afternoon I had a low. It wasn't a surprise. It happened most days but that day I texted my wife: "I just need to say this to someone, I don't want you to come and get me, but I've had enough. I don't want to sleep out tonight, I don't want to speak to another group, I want to be at home in a comfortable chair, falling asleep. I don't want to walk the remaining 25 minutes. I just want to stop." It was a Friday, though I'd lost track of the days, but there was no Friday feeling because being homeless means there is no weekend.

My wife phoned me and verbally picked me up and pushed me forward. Is that what I have done for the last 17 years? Is that what we do as essential services? Is that the foundation which allows health care, mental health care and other services to do their vital work? Maybe. Sometimes people tell us, "Without you I would be dead!" and I don't think I've ever appreciated that as much as I do at this moment in time.

Meeting people in the evenings has kept me going. Vital human contact, not a nod of hello as you pass someone on the street, but conversation, stimulation, companionship. Without that I don't know where my head would be. Without that, would the way I feel about myself be far worse? I suspect so.

Yesterday I walked past a little Sainsbury's in a nice middle-class suburb. I intended to go in, but a man was stood by the door with his dog and I thought he looked at me with disdain. It was enough for me to carry on walking. As I walked away, I laughed at myself. I could have stared at him with equal disdain, but I had felt judged. I had felt as though I didn't belong and even though I do, because I'm not homeless, homelessness is in my head.

> **I haven't enjoyed the last fortnight. I've loved meeting wonderful people and I've made some new friends. But homelessness got into my head and body and that's a horrible experience.**

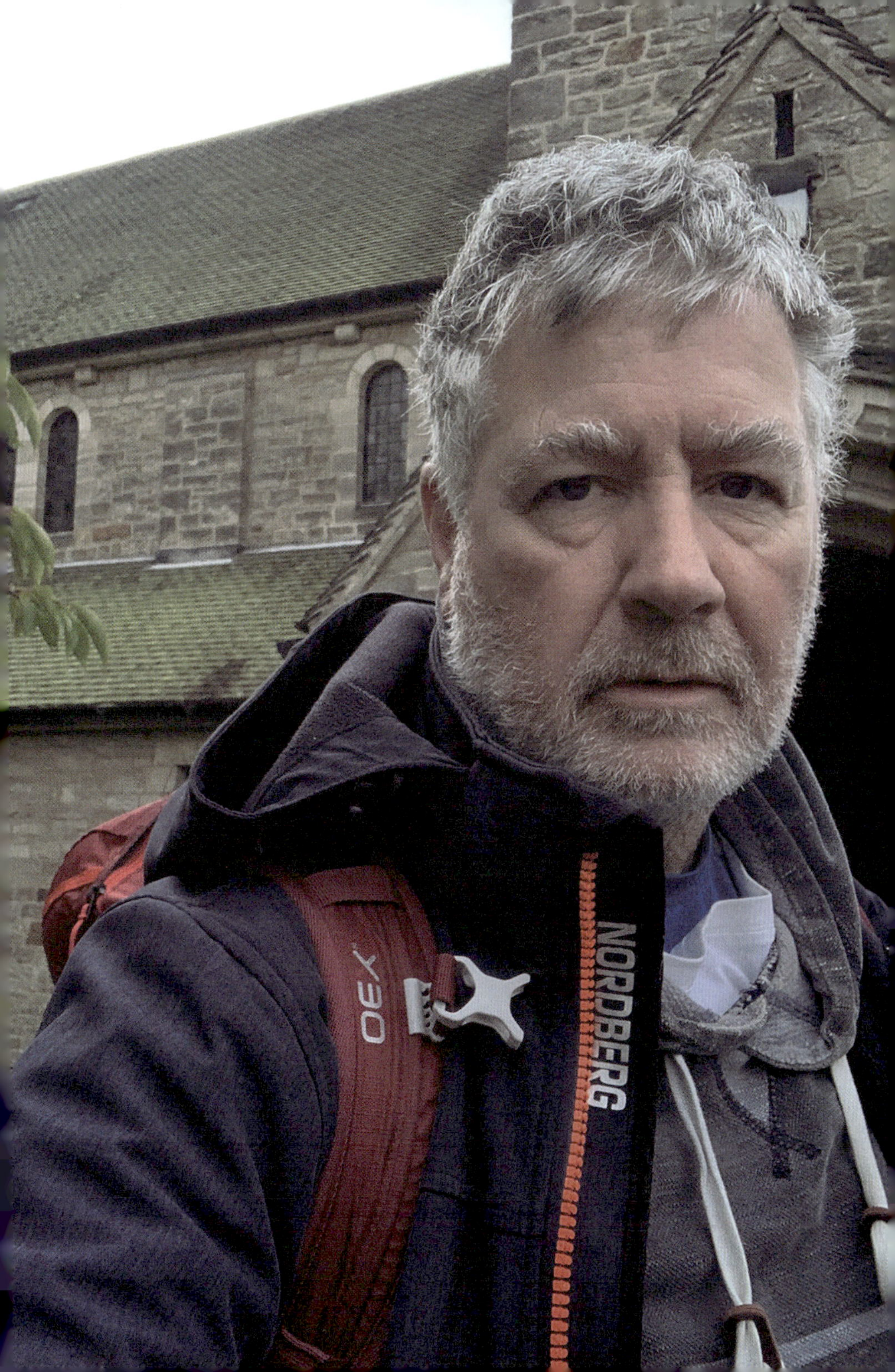
OEX 30
NORDBERG

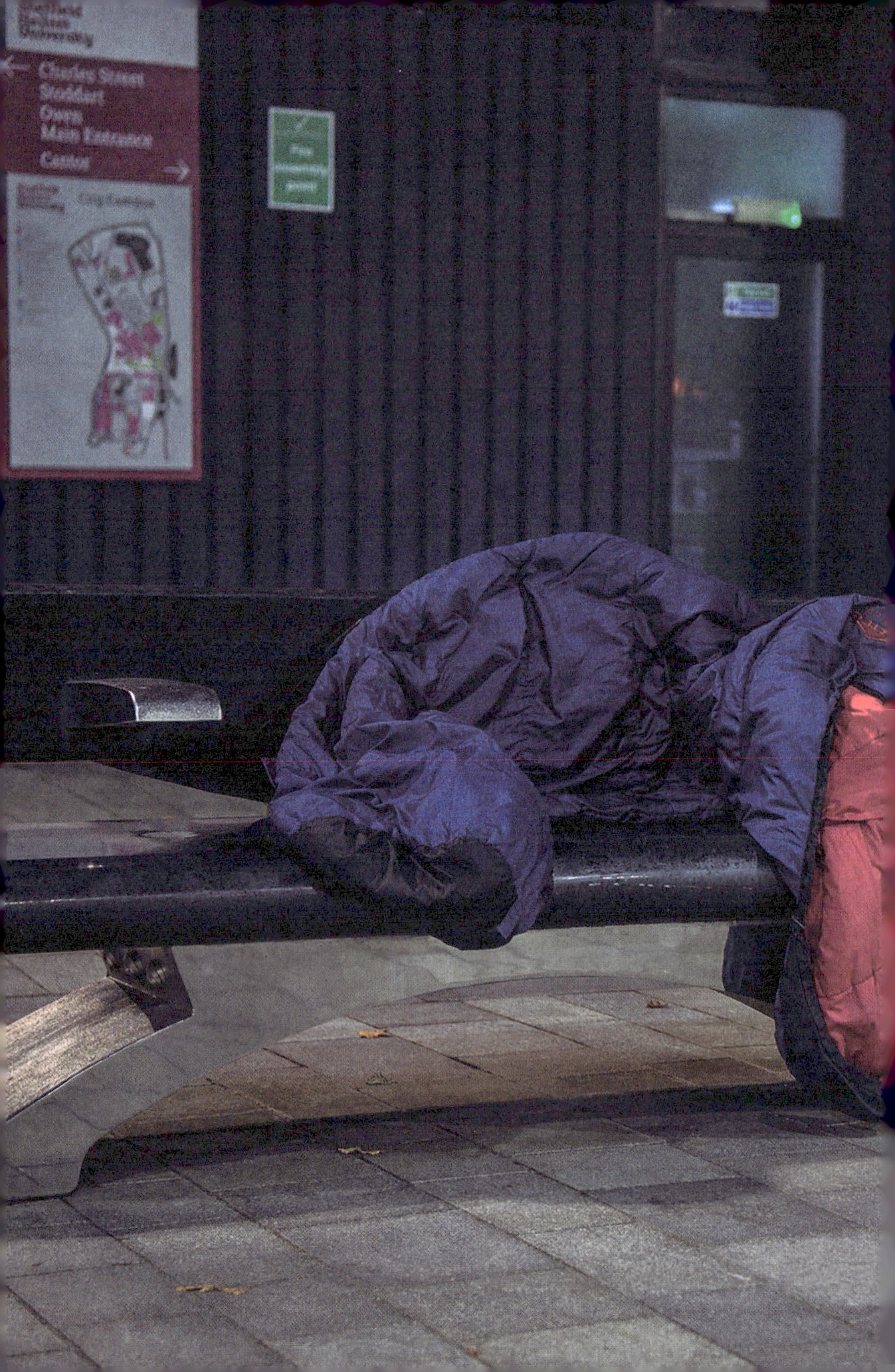
Charles Street
Stoddart
Owen
Main Entrance
Cantor

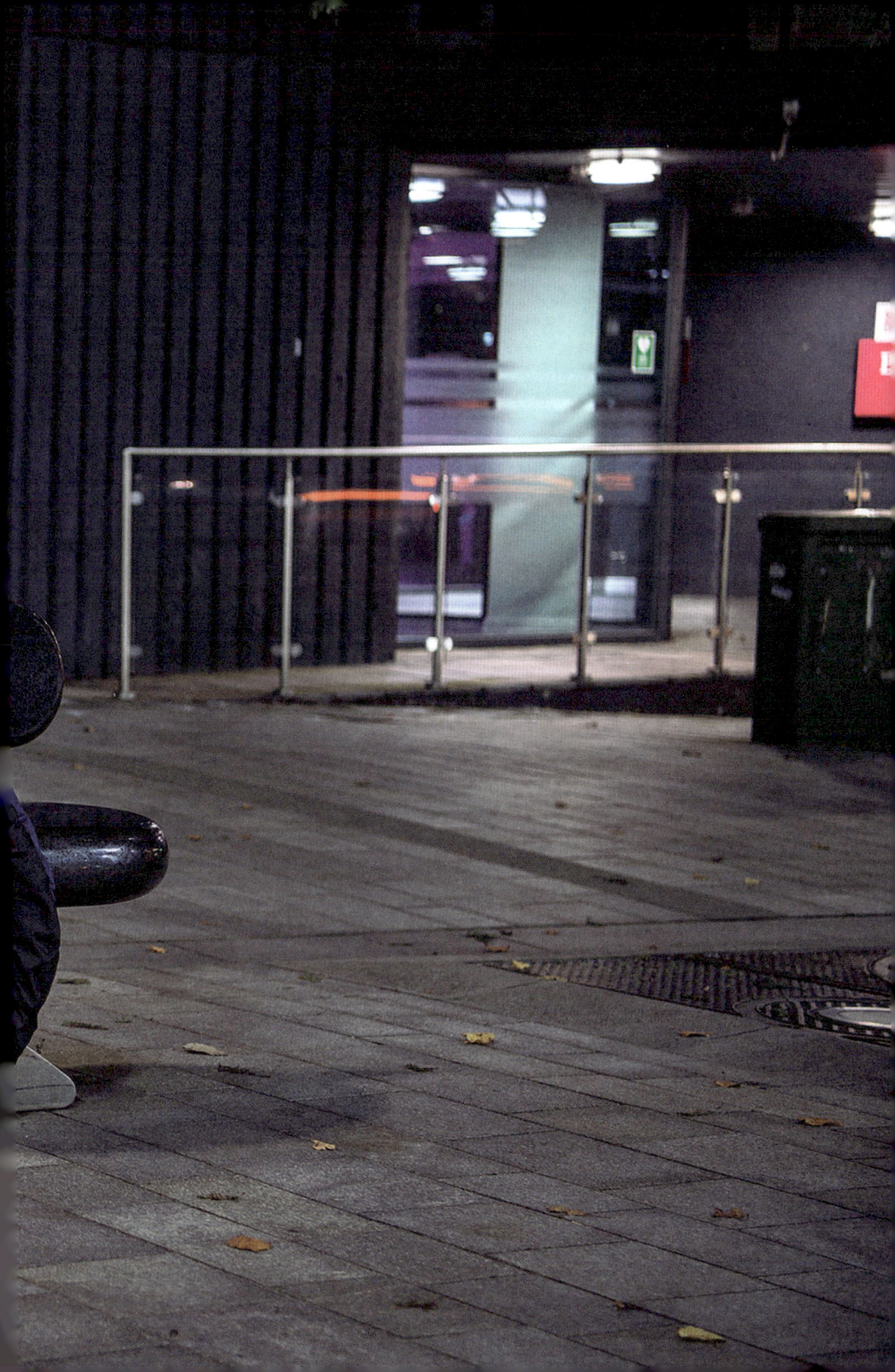

# Afterthoughts 1: Down but not out

**Yesterday was the kind of day I dreaded on my 14-night sleepout. The rain was heavy and incessant. I ran the short distance from my front door to my car, and at work, I ran from the car to the front door. Some of the places I slept would have been ruled out by yesterday's rain. The ground would have been soaked and I would have been stupid to sleep in places puddled with water.**

There are days at The Archer Project when we just need to make sure people leave with dry clothes. Keeping dry is part of keeping warm. If I had been sleeping out last night instead of last week, I'd have been huddled in the corner of a church porch, most likely sat up. And if I had got very wet during the day, I would have spent parts of the night walking around to create body heat.

People who sleep rough tell us about the cold and the wet, though very few words are needed. It's usually written on their faces and in their body language. A simple 'bloody freezing last night!' tells us they didn't sleep well.

I was lucky during my fortnight. Since getting home I've noticed how tired I have been. I'm a morning person; it's when I do my best work. I'm normally up at 6am, but not this week. My alarm went off and I reached for the snooze button, but I wanted much more than a snooze. I am still playing catch up, as I don't think I had one undisturbed sleep in those 14 nights.

Although I knew I was tired, I also knew I came alive when I met people. I enjoyed the companionship. Some people told me I looked better than they had expected. I meet people every day who summon the spirit to be cheerful. I know they are tired. I know they struggle with low moods. I know they have stories of serial abuse and neglect. I know the life they lead is incredibly poor. Yet somehow, maybe, hope remains. We see it in their humour, and in their appreciation (not every day) for what we and others offer.

Five days after my sleepout, I think it is this (sometimes hard to spot) hope that I find incredible and encouraging. An ability to defy all the negatives of life and get on with the next day.

> People who sleep rough tell us about the cold and the wet, though very few words are needed. It's usually written on their faces and in their body language.

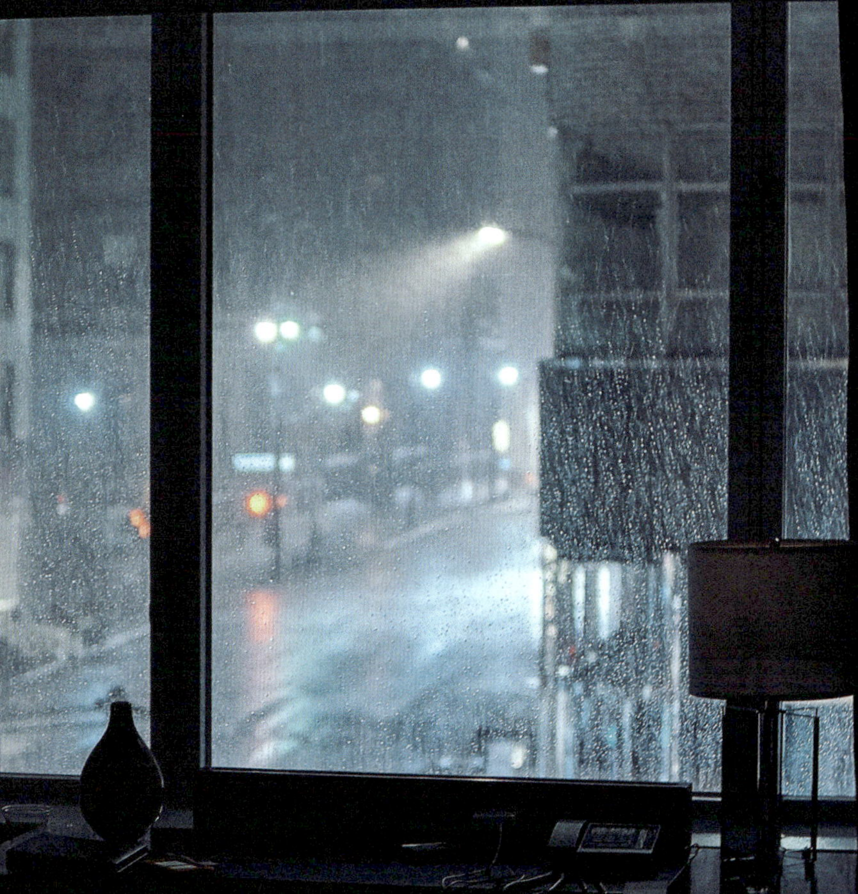

# Afterthoughts 2: Health and Wellbeing

On Saturday I had my Covid vaccine booster. On Sunday I had a headache. It wasn't terrible but it was persistent and neither paracetamol nor ibuprofen took it away. I ended up dozing on and off in the comfort of my bed or a large armchair. I had dreamt about the armchair when I was on the street. I had sat on pavements, on park benches, on upright chairs in popular burger chains or in churches. I missed somewhere comfortable to lounge. Towards the end of my 14-night sleepout, my back ached and my neck was getting stiff. My legs ached too, from all the walking. That's when I had thought of home and a large comfortable chair.

This may seem like a really obvious thing to say, but the street lacks some basic creature comforts. I had a really lovely shower at City Taxis' offices during my sleepout. I was very grateful. But it was a work shower. That means you get undressed in the little shower room, shower, dry yourself, and immediately get dressed again. It is efficient. It's not what I do at home. I sit, only half dry, on the edge of my bed and take my time. It's a creature comfort.

Everything on the street lacks comfort. Sleeping, sitting, dressing, changing clothes, cleaning: it is all grabbed whenever possible and it's basic. During my 14 days I was aware that I wouldn't normally neglect my feet in the way that I did. When walking in the summer, the first thing at the end of the day was to take my boots and socks off. But when I was homeless, the end of the day wasn't so clear. Bedding down isn't necessarily the end of the day. I realised that on my second night when I kept my shoes on, ready to move if needed. The nights were cold, and it seemed natural to keep my socks on most of the time.

I happened to meet a nurse who has worked with homeless groups for many years. He told me that foot care was vital. Athlete's foot, trench foot, and fungal infections are all well-known and just a stone's throw away from some regular creature comforts like fresh socks and washed feet. I never saw the need to encourage people to take their shoes off in the day before. That's changed.

But there is a wider point here. The creature comforts I longed for were about good health. Bad backs, aching necks, and sore feet are just the tip of the iceberg. Wet and cold weather have much more serious implications. And we haven't even mentioned mental health or the need to drown memories of past traumas in alcohol or drug use. The street is a health and wellbeing danger zone.

So now, with a minor reaction to a booster jab, I find myself asking: How would I cope if I was feeling this way and had no bed, no armchair and no home?

## Everything on the street lacks comfort. Sleeping, sitting, dressing, changing clothes, cleaning: it is all grabbed whenever possible and it's basic.

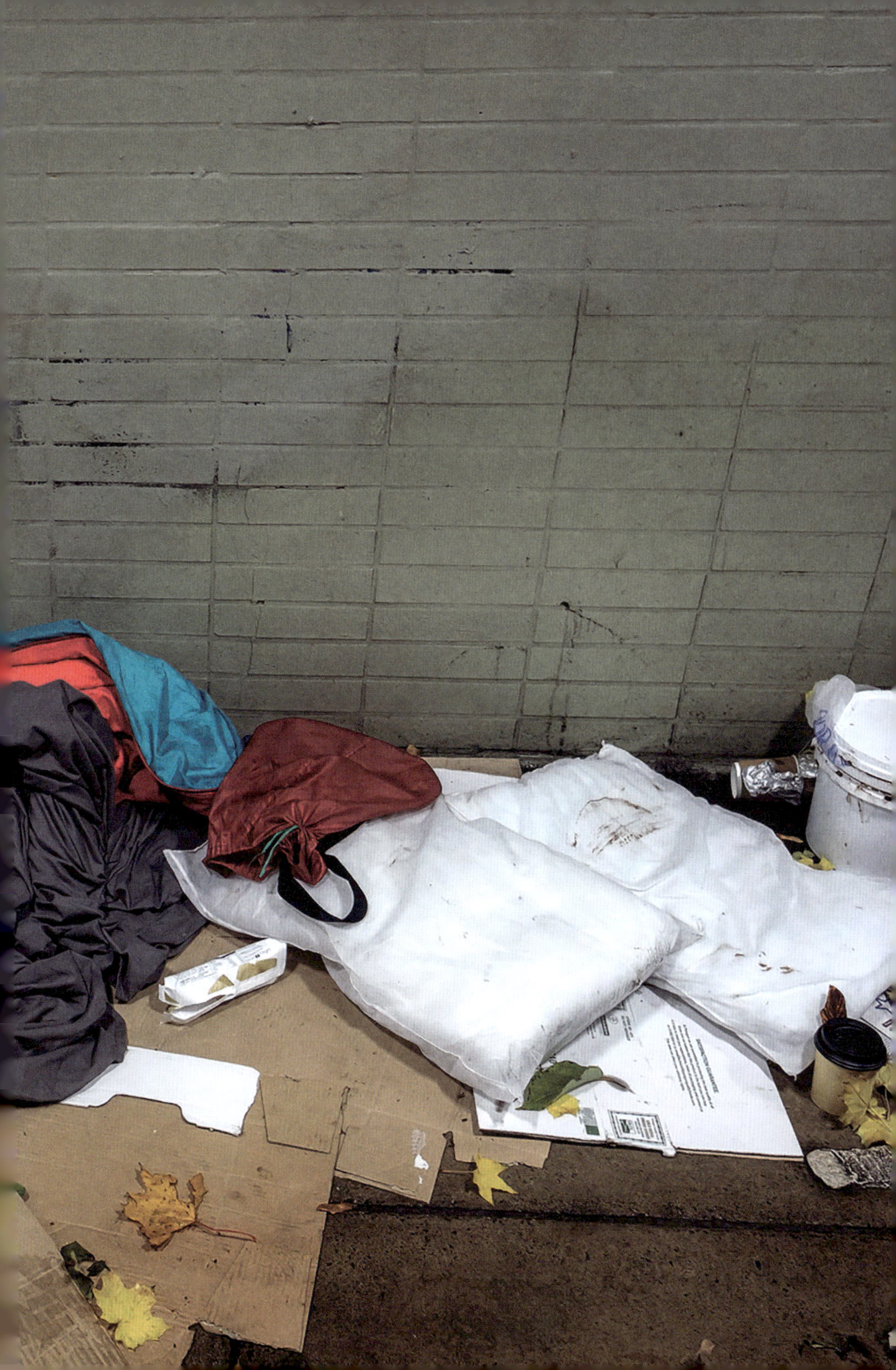

# Afterthoughts 3: Female Homelessness

During my fortnight on the streets, several women said to me that if they were to sleep rough there would be, as one woman put it, 'an extra layer of vulnerability". I realised that I hadn't ever considered the risk of a sexual attack on my sleepout. I've known men who have been sexually abused while sleeping rough, but they seem to be isolated incidents. I never considered it could happen to me. Women seemed to consider it automatically.

I am uncomfortable writing this. A 57 year old man sharing insights into being female and homeless? The reality is that I'm admitting my ignorance. After 17 years, I thought I knew the issues of female homelessness. I probably do, but I now realise how little I understand those issues.

I remember an incident involving a woman who was 19. She came to the project seeking help. Her boyfriend had been arrested. She was alone and said that, in the space of an afternoon, three men had offered to 'protect' her. She knew the cost of protection was sex with them and earning money for drugs by having sex with others. Shocking, isn't it?

I asked the opinion of women I know well who have experienced homelessness. One told me: "If you are a homeless woman, you expect to be offered something in return for sex." Her answer was immediate. She didn't have to think about it. For others it was being female that made them desperate to sleep on friends' floors rather than the street. Another, who had escaped domestic violence, simply said, "I couldn't do that. It was too raw for me." Her first response was to tell me why she avoided it, not that it didn't happen.

Near the end of my sleepout, I told a female colleague that I wouldn't want to be a woman on a period while sleeping rough. It is theoretical for me; I've no personal experience of menstruation. My colleague said, "Without medication I'd probably murder Bob [her partner] on a monthly basis. Have you thought about those women who have it really bad? Or menopausal stuff? And no medication?" No, I hadn't. And I find it difficult to imagine what 'really bad' really means. Aside from the physical symptoms, it strikes me there are other emotional and social implications I struggle to imagine too.

I'd mentioned menstruation because I wanted clean socks and underwear and thought clean underwear would be even more important for women. It was another colleague who said, "Yes, that's true, but some women want to be as unattractive as possible. A bad smell is a deterrent." Really? I hadn't thought of that either.

Of course, women speak to women about being a woman. I am on the outside. What is obvious is that I don't know the half of it, and this is too serious an issue to remain ignorant about.

> 'If you are a homeless woman, you expect to be offered something in return for sex." Her answer was immediate. She didn't have to think about it.

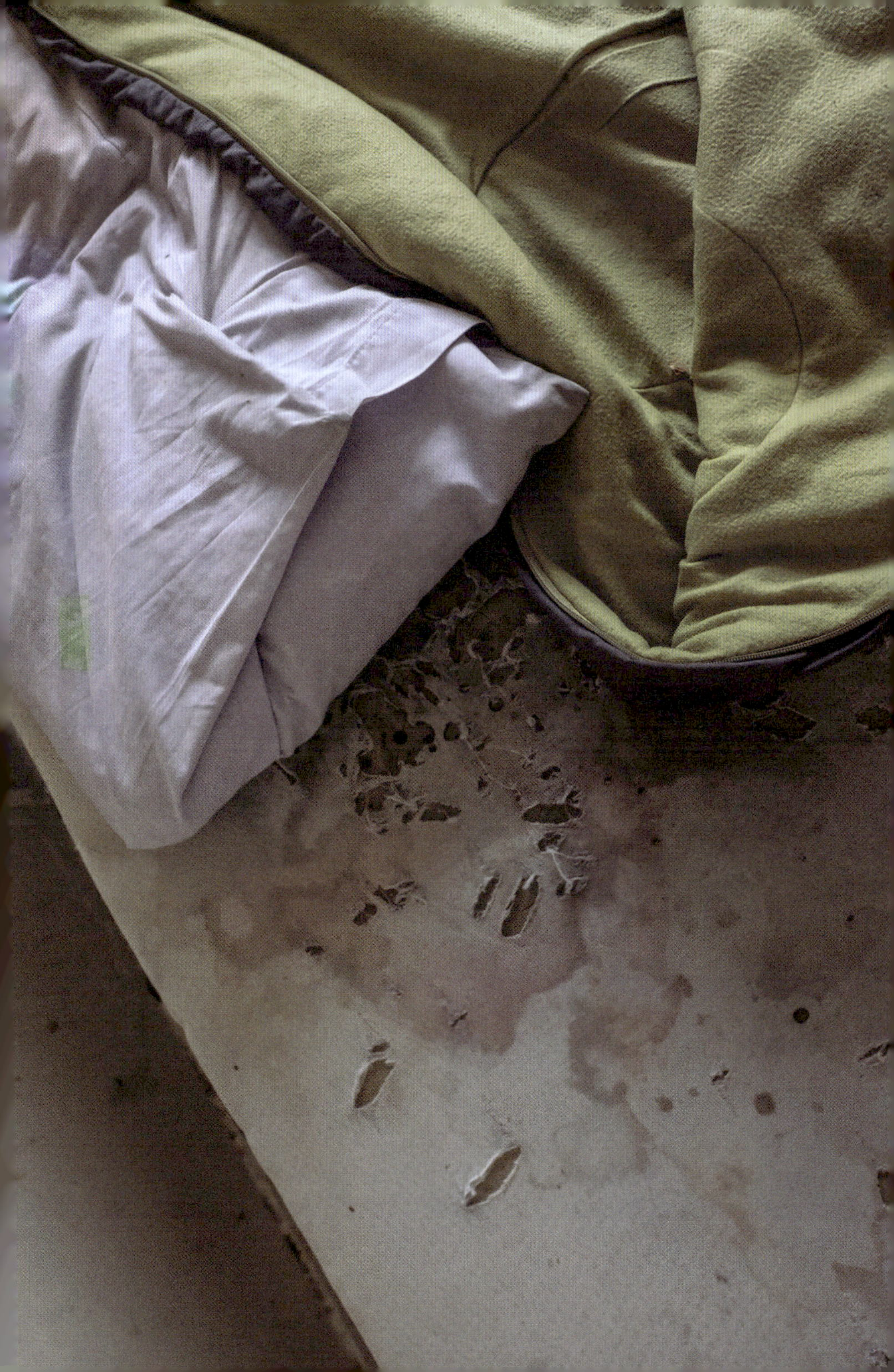

# REFLECTION

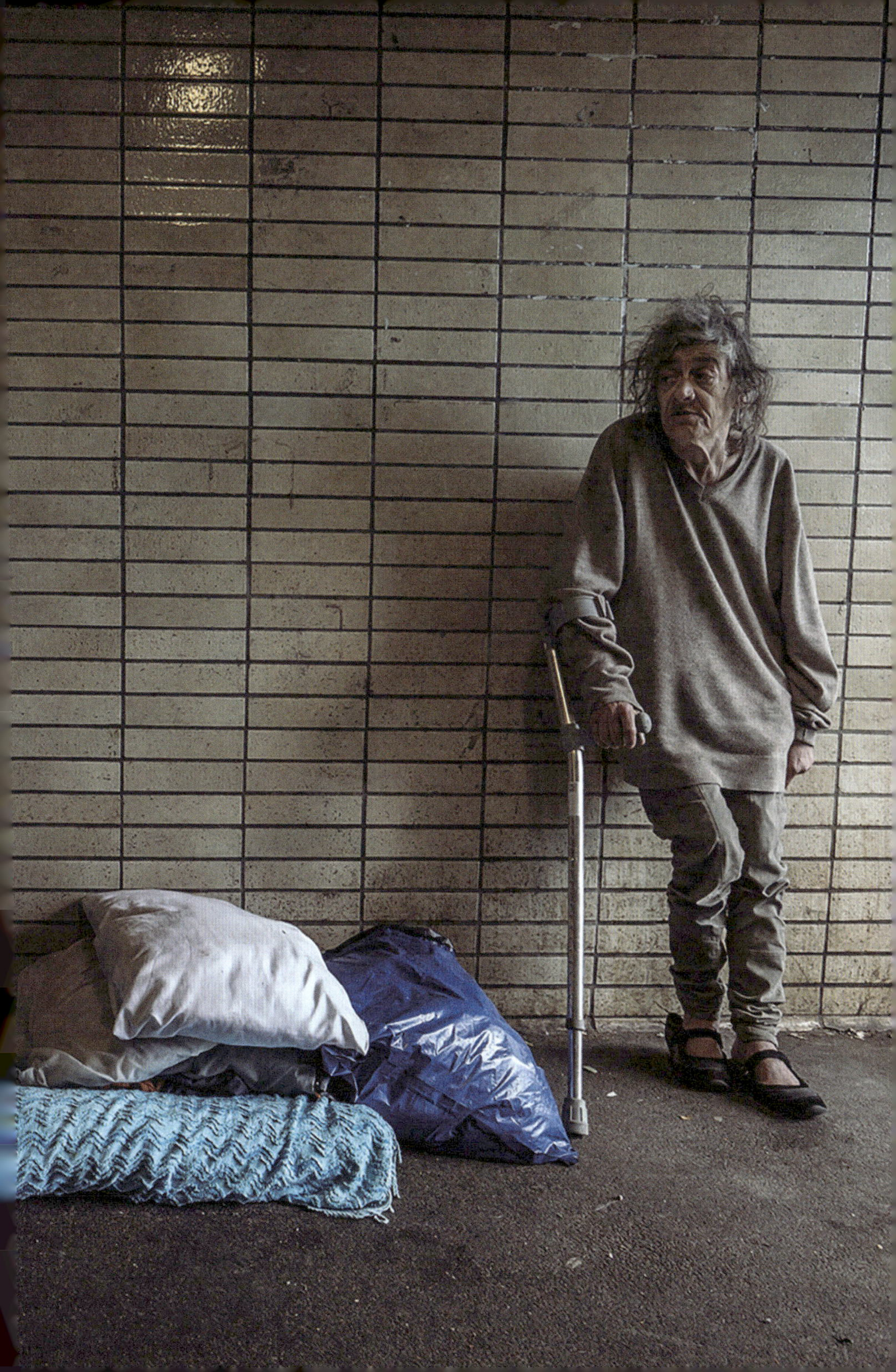

# F##k You!

"Have you recovered yet?" was the question everybody asked in the weeks following my sleepout. The answer was that it took no time at all to enjoy showers, access to the fridge, comfortable chairs, and a proper bed. The rest is up for debate.

James, a friend and former rough sleeper, took me for a debrief and I ended up wiping tears from my eyes talking through certain episodes of the journey. The problem is, I don't know how to share the power of the feelings I have been left with. The tragedy, it seems to me, is that the awfulness of rough sleeping is both obvious and totally hidden. I can see a person sleeping in a doorway and feel compassion or empathy. The journey that person went through to end up in that doorway and the longing that person has to be seen, heard and loved when they are telling you to f##k off, those things are anything but visible. But I believe we must learn to assume them.

In the middle of one afternoon on my sleepout, I needed the loo and set off for a local park. It's a large park so I figured it must have a toilet. As I walked through the park, I saw lots of people doing things I might be doing if I wasn't on my sleepout. Grandparents with children fresh out of school. Parents with buggies meeting other parents with buggies. People drinking teas and coffees in the lovely café. As for me, I was tired, smelly, and I believe I looked out of place. It felt wrong occupying space in that park. On reflection, I realised I was struggling with a deep-down feeling of resentment. I'd experienced it at other times too. I wanted what they had, and I resented them for having the freedom to be themselves. It wasn't about me having nothing. It was about feeling as though I didn't belong. I was alien to everybody else there. I was an outsider. That's what I resented. I didn't want any of those people in the park to not have what they had. I just wanted to belong there with them. And the feeling? I wanted to rage and shout f##k you. That's not language people would normally associate with me. I can feel it now and I imagine everyone who has been in that place feels it.

James listened and told me to multiply those feelings. He watched the world pass him by for years and noted that people didn't 'see' him when he needed them to, but last thing at night when he wanted to disappear to his private sleeping spot, he thought everyone was watching him so that his safe space would be compromised. A double whammy. Both visible and invisible, he knew he was excluded, disconnected from the things he wanted to be connected with. And he resented the world. But I believe the real truth is that if you don't belong to this society, you find belonging in another, and it is often destructive. It has its own moral code and values. Following the code takes you further away from belonging to our mainstream society. James described his escape from the dealers he owed money to, dealers who supplied the drugs that made life tolerable but who also made sure he was always in debt. As he spoke I could feel the anxiety within him, still real after all these years. It was a moment when he feared death and had to run and keep running. Sat on the street, as he was then, all of that was invisible to passers-by.

As we spoke, I wrote 'disconnection leads to resentment' in my notebook. A good while afterwards I realised there was more. Halfway through the sleepout I had sat and sobbed unexpectedly. It was provoked by such a small and seemingly inconsequential event. My phone had died during the day so when Gary, the vicar, met me at Wales Church, I plugged it in to charge. When I was alone again, I switched it on and heard it pinging repeatedly as it came to life. I looked at the messages; people were checking that I was okay. Seeing a message from my sister, I called her and as I commented on how people who are really homeless won't get messages asking how they are, or certainly not very often, the full force of that sadness hit me. Looking back, I realise that life on the street has a whole series of disconnections. Disconnection from the society around you. Disconnection from people you have known and maybe still love, whatever that love may look like. Disconnection from places that offer opportunities to grow employment skills and other social skills. Disconnection from facilities like electricity to keep phones alive and useful. That was the sadness I felt, the utter loneliness of homeless people, as if the world doesn't care. If that's the case, and I really think it is, isn't that something we have to change?

A few years ago, I was chatting to a man called Lee. He had paid work through one of our social enterprises and was good at his job. He related well to customers and he was proud of what he had achieved. I asked him why he had spent so long on the street. He told me that he thought he didn't deserve anything else, as if in the great cosmic plan he had been assigned 'homeless and addicted'. I argued back. I and some of our team had known him a good few years and had repeatedly encouraged him to look at different opportunities that existed. He said he knew that, but he didn't listen; he just said enough to give the impression of listening. Why? Because he believed he wasn't good enough. He believed he belonged on the street. To me it is the worst of all situations, disconnected and resigned to it. But eventually we offered something that caught hold of him and slowly over the next three years, his life changed from the street to employment and a sense of achievement.

Lee sits in the same category as the rough sleeper who joined me in Heeley and slept outside in the rain. In both cases a standard of life most of us can't conceive of was deemed good enough. How can that be? They may resent the rest of us for having the basics of life – the confidence to belong – but neither raged against it. Drugs and alcohol mask it, drown it, obliterate it, if only for part of the day.

In both cases there are tell-tale signs, often just a few words which hint at something sinister. "If I could cope with what my dad did to me, I can cope with anything." They were the words of the rain-soaked rough sleeper. Lee said, "Mum didn't want me in the house. I stayed with my grandma." It isn't my job to probe and question and tease out the details, but people share as they want to or feel the need to. Hopefully, one day they will get the chance to deal with those memories through therapy. Some will, others will struggle on.

The point is that so many people who become homeless have suffered severe or repeated trauma in their formative years. Carrie's story, which we've shared in this book, is awful but sadly it isn't unusual. The science is clear. Living through repeated trauma has a profound negative impact on the rest of your life, even in cases when the experience of trauma is used to teach or campaign or do something else that makes the world a better, more tolerant place.

As I walked to the city centre from Grenoside along the river out of sight of the busy Penistone Road, I was angry. Our government was in disarray, leaning ever more to the right and arguing for a smaller government. I wasn't aware of the ill-fated budget activity because I was avoiding the news but, on that morning, I was setting out my argument for a 'big enough' government. To argue small or large seems to miss the point. When children are repeatedly traumatised through abuse and neglect and we lack the resources to prevent that happening, then the government isn't big enough. Enquiries into the latest nightmare case are repeated but most cases of abuse don't lead to enquiries or safeguarding reviews. They happen because we have created a society in which they can happen. It has to stop.

How might we achieve that? Well, there is something that is evident throughout my blog. From before day one of my sleepout, the voices of people who are or have been rough sleepers were in my head and their influence lies behind every blog post. Before I started, when I thought that 14 nights wasn't that long, they told me I would learn a lot from the experience. They advised me and counselled me. They encouraged me and at the end they greeted me. But most of all they shared their experiences and I listened. I have always tried to listen and to value what is being said. I suspect that I listen differently now compared to 18 years ago.

The voice of lived experience is powerful and in it are the clues we need to work out a better way of protecting people from the experiences that lead to rough sleeping. Just listen. Not to one voice but to the many. They have the expertise to sit alongside the academic research and the skill of community, social, and health workers. In some cases, the lived experience and the academic researcher or health worker are one and the same.

All I know is that the more we involve, enable and empower people with lived experience to influence the way we work, the better we are at helping people to end their own journey of homelessness. In short, we can change 'f##k you' into 'that includes me too!'.

# The tragedy, it seems to me, is that the awfulness of rough sleeping is both obvious and totally hidden.

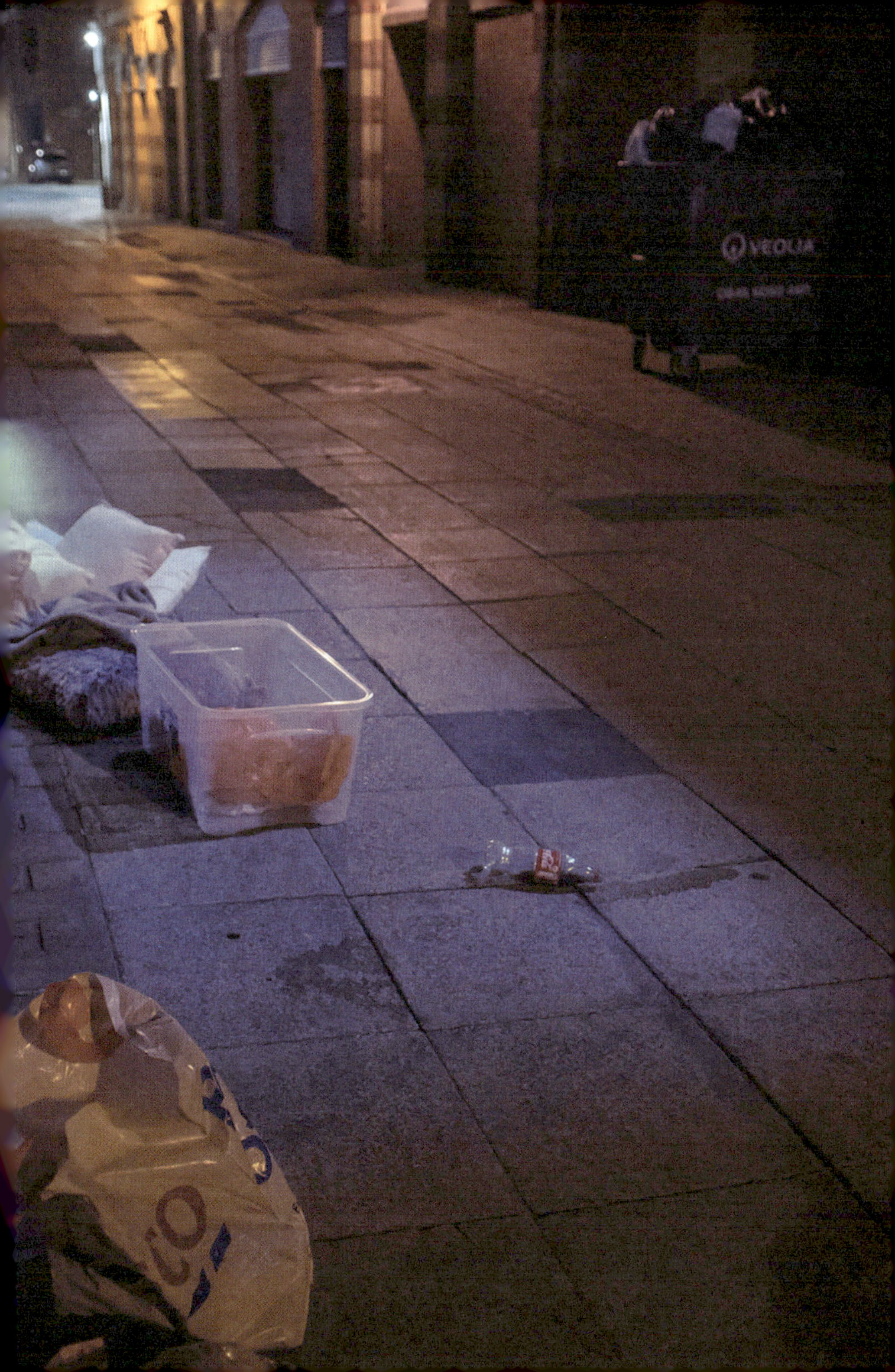
VEOLIA

'Thank you. So glad there wasn't another day to go. I really can't imagine how people make sense of the real thing. I really don't know what word to use: cope/survive/live…? None of them get to the depth of facing the repeated nothingness and sense of disconnection."

This was part of my response to James, a person with lived experience of street homelessness, the day after I finished my sleepout. He had sent a message saying well done. But I didn't feel I had done well. I just felt drained.

A few days later James told me I should debrief, so we went for coffee and I talked about key moments. I got a little emotional and he sat there and listened and then told me stuff about loneliness and loss, survival and celebrating small things as though they were incredible windfalls. We didn't take notes then but I knew we would sit together again and write down what he had said.

So, I asked others the same and Jo, Szymon, Andrea, Chris, Richard, and Carrie all took the time to tell me about their experiences too. These are the real stories of homelessness.

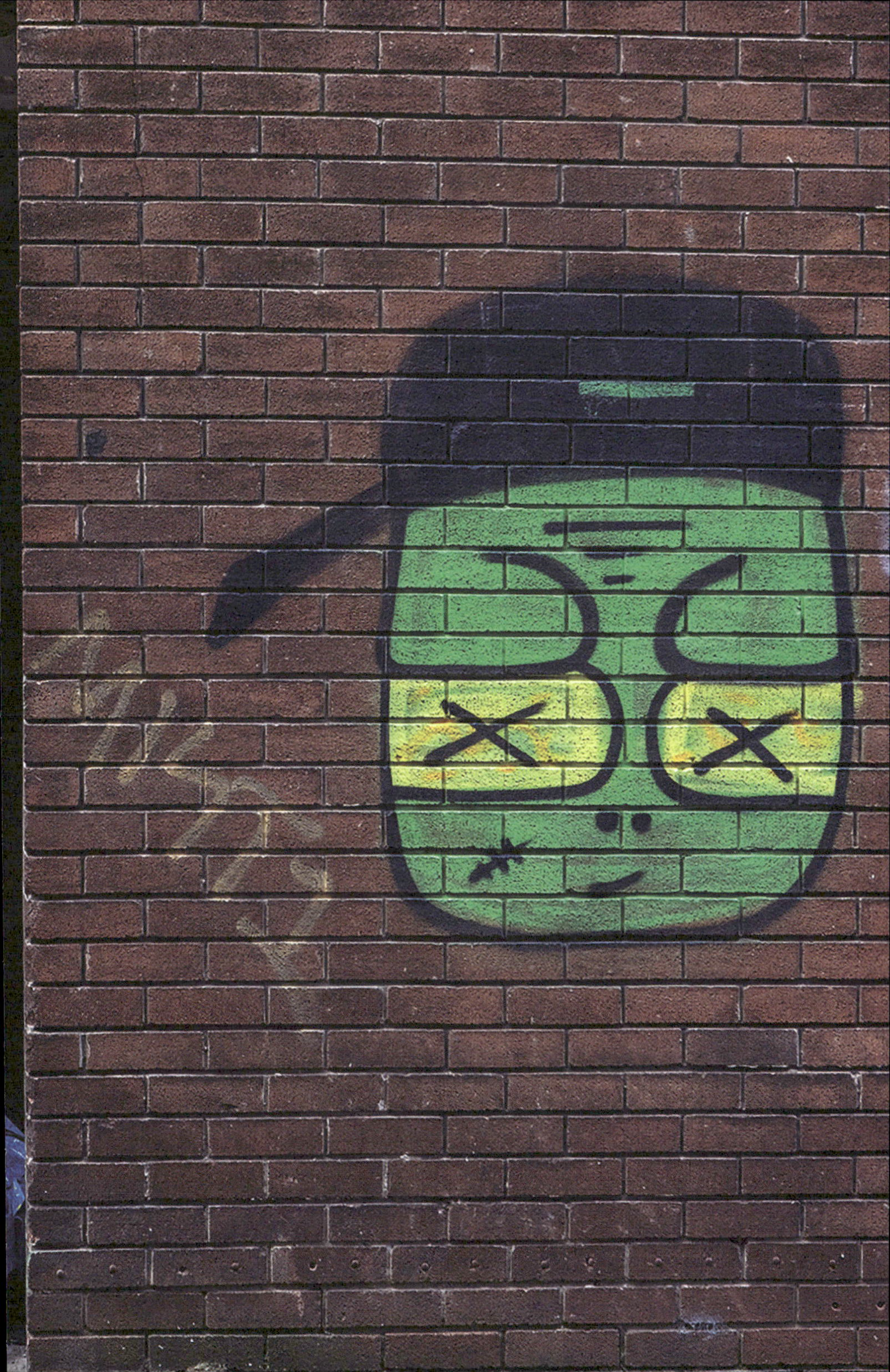

# James Creed-Gosling

**Day 1**

My own experience of the day that I became homeless is something I'll never forget. I wasn't prepared for losing my home. I had a home and then two hours later, I didn't. I left in fear for my own life and after the initial relief of having got away successfully, two hours later I sat in a forest on the edge of a park trying to process what had happened and that I couldn't go back. All the things you take for granted, I realised I no longer had. I was in shock. I left with a wallet and a cash card for an empty bank account having not eaten for five days. And I had to face up to the fact that this was a consequence of my own actions. I was alone, had nowhere to go and no one to trust, wondering how do I meet my needs, how do I eat, how do I stay dry, how do I find a safe place to sleep?

It's a massive thing to come to terms with. I didn't know if I would survive. Life very quickly becomes a series of carefully balanced choices. You lose a lot of your choices when you lose your home, and your survival depends on those remaining choices. On that first day, you haven't got time to process all that loss or all the feelings. I didn't have a tent. I didn't have a sleeping bag. My main concern was getting through the night and the next day. I sat there a long, long time in that wood. Eventually I had to get on with it. I didn't know if I was making good choices or bad choices. I just had to do something to survive.

**Day 2**

You become acclimatised to the lowest standards of everything. What you consider a normal night's sleep in a bed at home changes when you end up sleeping on the street. I used to be constantly trying to find ways to improve my makeshift bed; cardboard recycling bins were an absolute Godsend. Fresh, clean cardboard to insulate you and soften the ground, and yes, if only you had a pillow. I spent a lot of time rough sleeping and no matter what I got – a coat or a bag or some combination of stuff – it never ever substituted for a good pillow. It's made me very fussy about pillows now. They've got to be absolutely right for me.

There were times during my rough sleeping when I was able to hold on to a spot for many nights, sometimes weeks. Getting a good spot was important, and sometimes what looks like a good spot in the daytime changes at night because people's behaviour changes at night. People pop into places they wouldn't bother with in the daytime for makeshift toilets as they move from pub to pub, so you get used to not getting all your stuff out until it's really late and you think it's genuinely safe. You don't want to have to pack up and move on again. So, when you do find a good spot, holding on to it becomes imperative. A rule that I had was that if I did meet people in the day, even if I was drinking with them, I'd always be very careful to part company a long way from my spot because you never really know other people and I didn't want trouble from them or the people they were in trouble with. I shared a spot once and three blokes found him and beat him up. So, I would much prefer to be alone than face the consequences of other people's issues.

Familiarity is good too; a new spot comes with different noises. Is that somebody coming towards me or not? You learn to recognise the acoustics of a familiar place which allows you, hopefully, to get a good night's sleep, which when you're rough sleeping is a series of dropping off, going numb, waking up, turning over, dropping off, going numb, waking up, turning over, dropping off and repeating. You become used to that.

I smoked while I was a rough sleeper and soon became acclimatised to picking up tab ends. It was one less thing I had to raise money for, plus getting the tab ends and drying them out or just emptying them of tobacco gave me something to do. There are such long periods when you don't have anything to do or know what to do, and that filled a bit of time by keeping me occupied. It gave me a sort of sense of purpose that I had this process to go through and I had tobacco to smoke at the end of it. It was still a horrible thing to do. But you become acclimatised.

**Day 3**

People's reactions when encountering rough sleepers is fascinating. I spent a lot of time observing people and I saw so many different reactions. People seeing me in a doorway and shouting, "Sort your life out mate" or nudging their mate and going, "Look at him, dirty druggy". People make snap judgements about the situation I was in. Others would just walk by, not slowing their pace but saying something like, "Are you alright?". Sometimes they were the worst because I didn't need their pity; pity doesn't make you feel any better.

**Day 5**

There was a lack of purpose for me despite having stuff to focus on. There's a strange sense of achievement in getting through the rollercoaster of shoplifting, selling and buying: the sense that you have achieved what you need. It isn't really a pleasure but you're happy because you can relax. But the next day you have to do it all again because nothing lasted until the next day. A big pay day didn't last. If you get more money, you spend more on drugs and then you need more food. That was my experience anyway. It's an illness. If you have the drugs, you use them.

Getting a shower was very rare. It's so far down the list of priorities and where do you get one anyway? There weren't those types of services near me. I didn't know anyone who worked in a company who would let me come in and use their facilities.

**Day 7**

Staying dry limits you. You can't just walk. So, wherever you happen to be, you are at the mercy of whatever is happening in that place. You try and wait it out until the rain stops but there would come a point that you'd have to get wet because you don't want to miss your chances in the shops.

When I think through this, I'm thinking about a different me. I was driven by thoughts and feelings and having to use. That me didn't have a concept of not needing to use. There was no option at that time, not in my head. It was a must. So doing the daily work was a must and a wet day didn't stop that. You'd delay but there came a point when you'd have to get on with it because of the fear of ending the day without drugs. It wasn't going to come from somewhere else. I had to do it.

I look back on those times and I've got a very strong sense of that being the person I had been becoming for a long time. I didn't become an addict who was homeless overnight. It wasn't sudden. It had been a lifelong process. In some ways I know that I could still, very easily, be that person but I'm not because I've been through a process

# James Creed-Gosling (Cont.)

of learning about myself and the world around me through recovery. The things that stop me being in that negative place are things I work at every single day. It's self-management because I enjoy this me, I want to be this version of me.

This reflection is so difficult because it's taking me back into that life. I feel vulnerable looking back. It's scary. Doing this forces you to relive a combination of thoughts and feelings that feel dangerous. The emotions are so strong. I've struggled to do this. The only way I can grow is glancing in the rearview mirror. This is like looking in it for too long and I know that's when people crash.

**Day 8**

Phones are tools. You switch them on to ring a dealer and then you switch them off again. That's it. Preserving the battery is key. Relationships through messages, what's that? Relationships in the way we understand them are dead. And yes, I hated Christmas with a passion. I still don't like Christmas seven years on. I've seen a world where the ridiculousness of Christmas was put into perspective. I've sat watching people Christmas shopping, spending so much money and thinking, "You've got everything you need. You don't need more." I had nothing but the stress I saw in others seemed farcical. Why were people panicking and rushing?

**Day 9**

This was really interesting for me. The grief stuff. I think I'm someone who hasn't ever really grieved. I didn't grieve for my mum because I was so out of it. Grief is personal but it's also collective and I wasn't part of the family at that time. I just took more drugs to put the feelings of loss at a

distance and then eventually, looking back, I thought I'd gone through the process of grieving but it was only through coming out of homelessness and drug use that I realised I hadn't. I had to use counselling to go through it. I was about three months clean and had my first home, which I was on my way back to after a meeting, and I just started crying because I was thinking about my mum and the knowledge that she'd gone became a feeling. It had never been a feeling before. This is the point of drugs; this is why people take drugs. The high is opposite to pain and if you've got to the point where you don't know how to deal with emotional pain, you take drugs to get away from that pain.

What if? I've got more of an acceptance that for me personally there were many opportunities that could have stopped that decline, but I wasn't ready to use those opportunities. I think I had to lose everything. Only rock bottom could help me think about change. I was too scared to look at the stuff that would have been some sort of positive intervention.

**Day 10**

Over time, you forget those things that make up a 'usual routine' exist. You don't ruminate on those things. You just haven't got them. The counterbalance is that you become more excited about stuff you do have. The enjoyment of a cheese and onion pasty on the street was a delight. I celebrated when I got one as if it was a daily highlight or special event. With food, I had a self-enforced delayed gratification thing. I ate enough so I wasn't hungry but saved enough that it lasted all day, like giving myself rewards because I'd had the discipline to save the food and portion it out.

### Day 12

Rough sleeping vs sofa surfing. I've done both and been in horrific situations while sofa surfing because of not really knowing the people I'm staying with. Yes, you have a roof over your head, but you also have to live with another person's needs and perspectives and that can be dangerous. I was staying with one couple when the plain clothes police came to the house, but we didn't know what it was all about. Then I saw an article about the man. He had been jailed because he was a repeat sex offender. I didn't know that. He felt wrong but the risk at the time was irrelevant because I had a roof over my head. Now, I'd be following my gut feelings because I can afford to do that. There were times when the threat became so obvious that I'd go back to sleeping rough. That's the danger. You go into the unknown when you sofa surf. I used to pay the bloke in drugs because that's what it took.

### Day 13

I'd got really drunk by the canal in Chester. I met this random Russian guy, ex-forces. We were both drunk and he was challenging me to take him down. I ended up on the floor every time. When I woke up, I thought my ankle was broken. I walked to see a doctor. I must have stank, was hungover and in a terrible state, but the receptionist was fantastic. She cared for me, sat me down, made me a drink and the kindness broke through. I just cried. That kindness lives with you and gets you through the next days and tough times. It was the connection. Being treated as a human being.

### Day 14

It's amazing how long you can go without the loo! I think I went two weeks once. I remember trying to use the toilet somewhere but the security guard clocked and he stopped me going. Something about that experience meant that I didn't want to go through it again. I couldn't believe I was being stopped from going to the loo and then I just got constipated.

### Day 15

I went through that feeling countless times. Those are the days when you get arrested. You take less care because it doesn't matter. Those are the days you cry. If you get lifted you might get a place for a few hours, a microwave meal and a cup of tea. Strangely, you feel part of the system. You are paid some attention. You get to talk to people who want the details of your situation. They aren't going to do anything about it, but it is something different. It breaks your week up.

> **Over time, you forget those things that make up a 'usual routine' exist. You don't ruminate on those things. You just haven't got them.**

# Jo Leeming

One of the things to think about on the street is 'who will you see?'. It's the others who share your homelessness who will be your companions, and that's good and bad. They'll tell you how to get things, where to go for food and stuff. But really, they want you for what you might have. Money, drugs, knowledge. And for what you can offer. You'll be asked if you're on a script, which is shorthand for having access to drugs. They are not your friends, but they will be the best friends you have in that situation.

You don't buy cigarettes. Instead, it's dog ends from the floor or the top of a bin. I'd go through shop bins for food too. If I found really good stuff like bunches of flowers, I'd take them and sell them at the station. It all went into the pot for the drugs. At first, I used to think what I did was disgusting behaviour, picking up tab ends or raiding bins, but you soon get used to it and I made myself ignore the looks I got. My mum used to say I was disgusting, dirty and low. But I didn't choose to fall to the streets. When I first had heroin, it was the best feeling in the world, like living in a warm ball of cotton wool. The stuff that was killing me, the memories and thoughts, some of them to do with my mum and dad, just disappeared. It blocks all the bad stuff out.

I watch women getting bullied; one of them is getting hammered every day by her bloke. That shouldn't happen. That's what my life was like. I lived in this squat, Penny and Rob's Doghouse it was called. I stayed there because it seemed safer than the street, but it was far worse really. You had to go back with money and drugs, so I had to work during the day, begging, to keep my place. I remember a working girl there whose pimp came in with a gun. He asked her for drugs, she said no, so he shot her in the knees. You can't watch that and not be affected. It stays with me. It upsets me. Those girls work and get used and abused by the dealers and pimps. It shouldn't be like that. I lived in that culture. My stepdad had abused me, and I wasn't going to be abused like that again, but I was constantly told I could make money that way. A punter meant £20 for a stone. That's what I faced all the time. You could earn that £20, just like that.

I used to look at the couples holding hands. I watched them and thought about my kids. Everything seemed stacked against me seeing them. My ex-partner used to tell my kids all sorts, filling their heads with stuff I've never done just so they would hate me. He'd give me money because he knew I needed my fix, on the condition I wouldn't speak to my kids. Christmas was horrible. Just so lonely. HARC provided dinner but it doesn't fill the gap, the need and want to be with people you've lost, when you know they're somewhere doing Christmas without you.

There should be more places for rough sleepers. They shouldn't be in the wet. We'd make shelters out of bin lids and wrap them in cardboard. All the empty buildings in town, why can't they be used?

Toilets were a big thing for me. Finding somewhere in the city centre to go for a pee was a nightmare. I used to get turned away from cafés, so it had to be alleys. Maintaining privacy was a big thing. No-one is there with baby wipes. And blokes follow you to take advantage. I see it happening today and I can spot it because that was my life. It's still some of the same blokes doing it.

You aren't a woman on the street. You're just homeless. As a woman I just wanted love, a hug, some gentleness and recognition, but there isn't any. If you go to J--- [a known dealer] with a pound for drugs you'd come back with no knickers. He'd have his way somehow. It costs you big time.

As for medicine, I didn't bother with it. Your addiction is the most important thing and the second and third most important things. I was picked up and taken to hospital with heart failure and then, once I was in hospital, I got pneumonia. I was put in a coma to recover. But I didn't care about my health, not at the time.

Has it ended yet? Well, I think it never really ends. I've got a home, I've got a different life, but that homeless life stays with you. I live in two worlds. I've had to build bridges with people, including some of my family who I still don't really like because of the past but the alternative is awful loneliness. When I'm in town now, I watch the street and look at what's going on, because I know it's doing to others what it did to me. It's almost like an addiction; I can't stop watching and worrying over people. So no, it never goes away.

I hope homeless people get the justice they deserve and one day we'll be treated as equals.

> **I used to look at the couples holding hands. I watched them and thought about my kids. Everything seemed stacked against me seeing them.**

# Szymon Slotwinski

There weren't many places I could go into as a rough sleeper. That's why I came to The Archer Project, because I could do things there. I played football. The massages were the best. Posh people pay lots of money for that; we could have it and get dinner afterwards. In your head you tried to deny the reality, telling yourself "It's not so bad. It's not dire straits." But it was that bad. I sold the Big Issue and got some money so the negotiation in my head about how bad life was could go on. I wore some strange clothes at times. I remember wearing this big fisherman-like raincoat and people would look at me strangely, but I would look back at them. You have to make yourself special somehow in order to survive. Homelessness is not only having nowhere to sleep, but also nowhere to go. Without that you can't feel normal. You are on the streets, so I went to drink with friends on the street rather than sitting on my own. Having a place is important.

You compare yourself with other people and you get jealous. I fancied a woman who worked at The Archer Project in those days and I thought, "if only she knew that I was homeless because something happened to me accidentally, and I was really okay..." but the homelessness was real and that put a block in the way of her seeing me differently. If she had seen me at the university a year earlier, she would have seen a different person, in my eyes anyway. Instead of helping me get out of homelessness, maybe we'd have talked about other things, and I would have had more dignity. So I felt jealous, upset and angry, regretting my past and feeling that I had failed in life. It is not easy.

Using the phone at The Archer Project to contact my family was how I got to know Terry [a support worker at the project who was instrumental in helping Szymon move into employment]. I talked to my mum and she knew something was wrong, that I wasn't happy, but I spared her the details. I was glad I did that because when she found out, much later, and she watched something that had homelessness in it, she told me it made her think about me. I used to tell her it wasn't so bad, that I had friends who helped and a good place to sleep and things like that.

You have to accept you are homeless, yes, but to cope you can flip it. At times I used to look at people and tell myself I was better than them. You don't have a flat, you don't have a home, but you can drink whatever you want and you don't have responsibilities, so you can make yourself think it's the others who are trapped rather than you, because for a while it helps. I wouldn't think that way if I wasn't homeless, but I had to make my situation bearable.

I don't know where the energy comes from; you are constantly vigilant, aware of places where you might sleep. Your mind is constantly working too; I would think about my debts and the bank, for example. It is completely exhausting. So, you have to be strong and have endurance and be brave to survive on the street. I tried to convince myself it was something else, like camping, but it wasn't. So, I would get a book and a bottle of cider and drink to cope and to survive.

I met with some friends who are all former rough sleepers and we talked about Tim's sleepout. He did okay, seriously, but he didn't have a habit to feed. So he didn't spend his days trying to get alcohol or drugs and that's very different. That's what we had to do, and it's hard. And when he talked about home, we didn't have that. We didn't have a picture of what home looked like. It was a definite place for Tim, and it was definitely going to happen. It was just an idea for us, and we didn't really know how it would happen or even if it would happen. That's what it's really like.

**You have to accept you are homeless, yes, but to cope you can flip it. At times I used to look at people and tell myself I was better than them.**

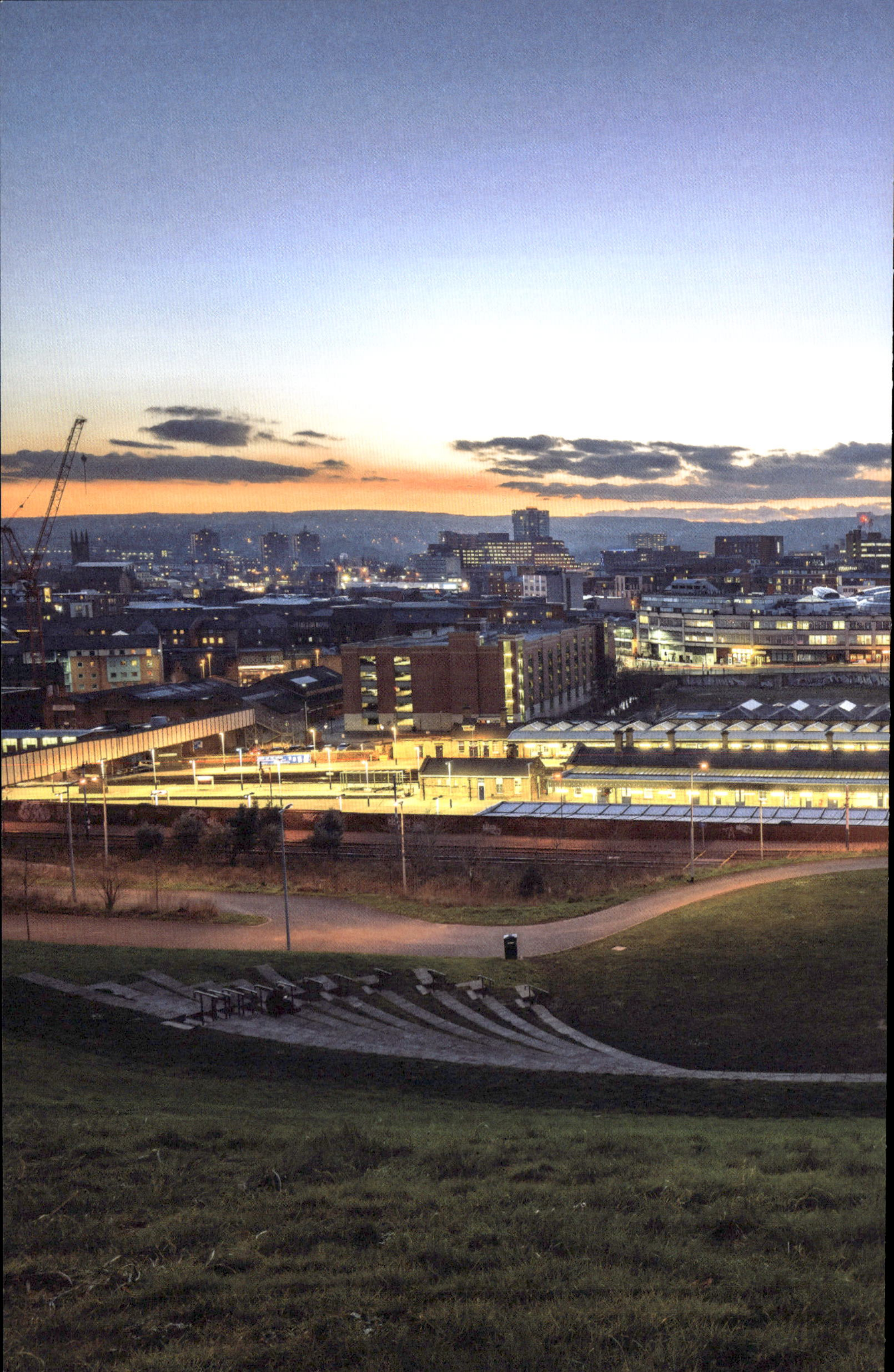

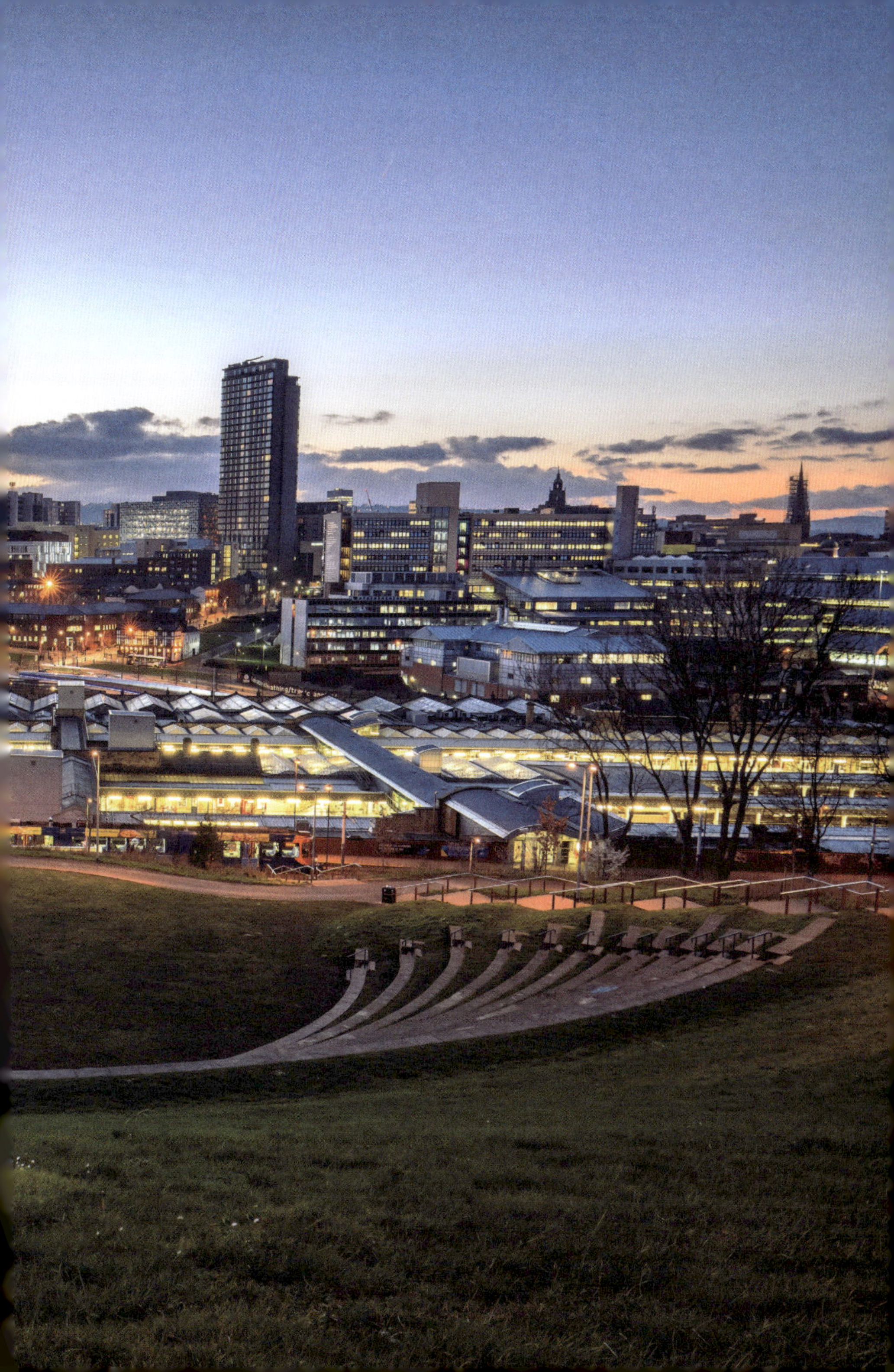

# Andrea Fowler

My homelessness began when I was 14 and it all started with rebellion against my parents. Mam and Dad wouldn't let me sleep at friends' houses, but I thought "sod them" and went to stay with a friend anyway. One night led to two nights, then to three, and by that time I was too scared to go home because I knew I was going to get into trouble. Maybe a couple of nights later it was, "You're going to have to go home now Andrea, it's getting a bit much." So I went and found somebody else's settee to sleep on, and if not, I went to a graveyard, though I never actually slept there because it was too scary with all the noises.

When I was homeless it was pre-mobile days. I had to go and knock on people's doors, fingers crossed hoping they would be in. I tried not to think of my mam and sisters. Just thinking about where I was going to stay that night took all my thinking. I'd try one place after another and nobody would be in. At some point one of them would get back home and I'd just sort of hope they might say, "Do you fancy staying tonight?" Happy days if they did, not so happy if they didn't. I'd be knocking on doors up to 11 at night, just hoping. Otherwise, it would be back to my graveyard, as I called it, at the church. It took a lot of effort to knock on people's doors, thinking of things to tell them so you can actually get inside – you know, "I thought I'd pop around to see how you are and have a chat." – and hoping to God they wouldn't say it's time to go now. If they did, that was it. I fell apart and knew I had to go to my graveyard.

I thought my mam and dad didn't love me, that they didn't even like me, because my dad once asked me, "Is there owt wrong with you?" I said no, and he said, "There f###ing is because you're breathing." That hurt me, and I think that when he shouted at me it all built up and leaving home was a way of getting back at them. I didn't think they'd be bothered anyhow because they didn't love me and they didn't want me there. That's one of the reasons I didn't think about them.

Shame meant that I got to the point where I couldn't go home. I didn't go to the town centre just in case somebody would see me who knew me, or knew my parents. The last thing I needed was to bump into one of my family members and then they'd go and tell my dad I was camping out in the graveyard. I had to avoid areas where others would be, so I felt as if I had to be on my own. It's really hard to explain how I felt. I had all sorts of different emotions and feelings going round and round. And I was young. I was still learning.

I never got to the point of thinking, "I don't give a toss about what people think of me," because I wanted people to like me and that's why I found it really hard to say no to people, because if I did, they wouldn't like me. Later, I had to do stuff to get places to sleep, sex stuff. I didn't think I could say no; they were giving me shelter, after all. When I did say no, it might happen anyway – even in the middle of the night when I was asleep. Being taken advantage of like that takes its toll, and I lost a sense of what was good for me. I just wanted people to like me, so I slept with a lot of men hoping for something good.

I got to the point where I'd run out of places to stay. I was tired and hungry and fed up. Nobody loved me, everybody hated me. I actually walked to Clive Sully [the road that leads to the Humber Bridge, where Andrea lived in Hull] and I thought about it, but I didn't have the bottle to do it. I really didn't have the bottle and that's what stopped me, not anything else, not the thoughts of what it would have done to my family. I took an overdose of 75 paracetamol but didn't hold them down. I was so lonely. I thought nobody loved me and the best place for me was to be gone. But now, I am so glad I didn't carry it through.

**One night led to two nights, then to three, and by that time I was too scared to go home because I knew I was going to get into trouble.**

# Chris Lynam

Tim's blog was a fascinating read for me, and others' reactions to it have surprised and fascinated me in equal measure. Some people felt that he wasn't really homeless during the sleepout, which I don't completely agree with. I used to be homeless and have worked at The Archer Project for years now. Once upon a time – actually just six short years ago – I was released from prison, homeless and a former heroin addict. I was lost. I had a difficult childhood with predictable results, much like lots of us here.

I met other 'Tims' on the street too, men who technically had a home but whose marriages had broken down. Having been cohabiting with their partners and children in the family home, those men had chosen to make themselves intentionally homeless so as not to upset their kids' lives even further. Doing this had made them un-housable in the eyes of their local authorities, despite these being people who had worked and paid taxes all their lives and contributed positively to society.

Tim is of course not homeless, but in my opinion he was then. Sure, he had a shower once, churchyards to sleep in and some basic provisions. But the sleepout was not about proving how authentically down and out Tim himself could get. This was an experiment to understand from a psychological perspective what people who have experienced homelessness on our streets feel.

The worst part, personally, about becoming homeless was the beginning, that jarring adjustment to the vulnerability and discomfort of your new surroundings. To leave the warmth and security of your accommodation rapidly and be thrust into this hazardous and frightening new world. It was the realisation that although I was never a big fan of people or crowds, I had been part of a tribe, this society of ours. Once I became homeless, I was exiled, excommunicated to the other world, much like Tim and some of the other people he spoke with on his journey.

Quite soon into that journey, you see how the alienation of homelessness begins to affect one's soul. Just like us, Tim's behaviour and thought processes began to change in accordance with this new self-image. A good example of that contrast is the veteran rough sleeper snoring loudly, fast asleep in the same position he laid down in, while Tim is unable to sleep in the cold and wet weather. Other than a comfortable night's sleep, you also lose confidence – helped along no doubt by stinking feet and unwashed clothes – which further lowers your self-esteem and makes you feel unworthy.

The end of the blog was the most striking for me. Tim was miserable, his immersion complete, fighting within himself about whether to enter a shop where people may or may not be judging him. We learned a lot from the way experiencing homelessness left a mark on Tim, or at least we should have done. If we didn't see how much the sleepout negatively affected him – not just how uncomfortable and cold and miserable he became but also the emotional and mental toll – then in this writer's opinion, we may have missed the point. Think about how a well-adjusted, sensible and resilient man with experience in the field of homelessness, a job, a home, a supportive and loving family, who had all his immediate basic needs met and only removed temporarily, was still brought so low by those two weeks, even with the knowledge that it would end.

Now can you imagine how a human being feels when they are trapped there for months, years, or decades with no end in sight?

**The worst part, personally, about becoming homeless was the beginning, that jarring adjustment to the vulnerability and discomfort of your new surroundings. To leave the warmth and security of your accommodation rapidly and be thrust into this hazardous and frightening new world.**

# Richard Allen

I needed to make money. In some ways that filled the day: getting money, getting a fix, getting high. I spent most of the daytime asleep because I was a night-time earner. First thing I'd do was get money for a bottle of sherry. That would take the edge off, so the feeling of illness would go away. I'd drink it straight away. If I'd got enough money, I'd buy two and make the second bottle last. Then I'd tap enough for some drugs – a mixture of crack and heroin – and that would stop the rattle I had. Basically, just like the sherry, I'd feel better and be able to function. Then I'd beg a cigarette and go out to beg. I judged everything by how much money I could make. The more I made, the more drugs I could have, the more I could get away from reality. I had no problems in life when I was high. When I wasn't, all life's problems were there.

Where did my pain come from? Not having a family, not being loved. I was bullied. I expected to be bullied. I expected people to not want me around so I escaped as much as I could. I didn't hate myself, I hated being me. I hated all my younger years. I hated not being able to understand what happened. I think too much and it was all negative, horrible stuff. The drugs stopped that.

Tim describes looking around him during his sleepout and wondering about other people he saw, what they were doing, where they were going. I was way beyond that. For me, people were to be avoided or they were an opportunity for money. It was black and white. I wouldn't sit there thinking 'I wonder what they are doing?' and I didn't give a damn about what they thought of me. I liked it when someone chatted to me though. It made me feel as though I fitted in, if only for seconds or minutes. There were a few workers, drugs workers and the like, who I got to trust but I found that awkward. I had to test them. It was strange liking someone. But I don't think I'd be here today if that hadn't happened. It took a long time for me to get that they believed in me.

On Day 13 of his sleepout, Tim saw someone he knew and he "came alive". I'd be the opposite. I didn't want to see people from my past. I didn't want to hear how well they were doing and stuff like that. I didn't want them to see what I'd become, how far I'd dropped.

Tim had a plan. He knew where he was going to sleep. I didn't plan. There was a pattern of going back to the last place I'd slept but someone might be there, and I'd have to go somewhere else, or I'd meet someone with a chance to share drugs or alcohol and go with them. It just was what it was.

I survived on quite little food. When I was hungry, I'd go to The Archer Project. Or we'd find bins full of good food. For a time, a Chinese buffet left stuff at the end of a night and that was good. But food was quite low down my priorities. I managed to get some food most days.

I got used to not having toilets but that's not nice and I made myself poorly a few times trying to hold it in because I wanted a loo. When you look homeless your face doesn't fit and shops won't let you go. Security turns you away or staff tell you toilets are for customers only. I'd go to a proper loo if I could sneak in. Pubs were the best bet. Otherwise, you find an alley.

Keeping dry in bad weather as a rough sleeper is massive, but for me it came second to earning money. I needed drugs so I'd go to bed wet if I had to. But then I was taken to hospital because I got so cold one night and it turned into pneumonia. I remember an outreach woman bringing clean socks and baby wipes once. That was wonderful. I cleaned my feet and then put socks and shoes back on. My socks were usually disgusting because I walked loads and never left my shoes off.

Feeling safe is important. I felt I developed a sixth sense, as if constantly aware, even when I was out of it. But you develop behaviours that are about safety too, which is why I'd never leave my shoes off. I was always ready to run. But that doesn't mean you are safe. Tim spoke about women being more vulnerable and that's right. Absolutely right. But men get sexually attacked too. I did, when I was asleep. And I wasn't alone, so I should have been safer. I woke with a bloke on top of me performing a sexual act, let's leave it at that. It took me ages to get over that. I felt levels of self-loathing I'd never felt. I never thought it could happen to me. I spiralled big time, more drugs than ever. It sounds stupid because you don't sleep well on the street. You're always tossing and turning because of the pain of the hard ground on your hips and the noises that sound wrong and wake you. So, sometimes I took sleeping tablets. I had that night. I hated myself.

Tim only took stuff that rough sleepers have but he picked them out and prepared himself. Life on the street is usually more opportunistic. If you get a sleeping bag, great. If you get a tent, bonus. But it wasn't like that most of the time. You got what you could get to make a bed. If you got lucky with good stuff it was like hitting the jackpot. Compared to the rest of the world you've got nothing, but you feel so happy, even if it is for just a few hours. It sounds weird but I can picture myself now, extra thick cardboard mattress, good food from a bin, lighting a roll-up and saying, "This is the life."

There was an incident in a fast-food place when Tim felt he was being watched. That's so real. I felt monitored everywhere and that's why places like The Archer Project are so important. You can go in there and feel welcomed. It was the only place that gave you that, and they did stuff for you. It felt like my space when I went in. Back on the street, I lived in a different world to the people around me. I didn't fit in, and you feel like people have got eyes on you, judging you, rejecting you, laughing at you, sniggering at you. Tim writes about his 'f##k you' feeling but I know he also wanted to say 'if only you knew me' because he wasn't really homeless. Well, I felt both of those. "What are you looking at? F##k off!" was just a repeated thing but I also wanted to say, "I can be more than this, much more than this, if only you'd help me." But back then I didn't trust anyone to help me. Finding that person seemed impossible.

I got off the streets, but it wasn't because a group of trustees turned up with breakfast. In the end I got clean. Clean is free from drugs and alcohol. That meant I could do things, sort housing, be human. Think. Function. Live. I went to a B&B and I can't remember the precise series of events but I made it. Life is good, though I still struggle to sleep well in a proper bed.

# I liked it when someone chatted to me though. It made me feel as though I fitted in...

# Carrie

My dad was a violent man when I was younger, so the abuse started when I was a baby. I was malnourished when I was a kid; my mum and dad would sit on the sofa eating steak while me and my brother were eating pizza crusts from two days ago.

I was four when my brother started sexually abusing me. He was seven. It started when my mum got us a babysitter who turned out to be a prostitute. She was bringing punters back to our house and that was where my brother learnt that behaviour.

My brother went to live with my nan and my mum ran away to Lincolnshire where she met another man. On their return, we all went to live in Maltby. Three weeks later I was raped when I was walking back from a friend's and cut through a graveyard. I wasn't even nine years old at the time. There was no conviction.

I went into care when I was nine. My mum didn't even tell me I was going into care; she said I was going on holiday for a couple of weeks. I wasn't the easiest kid. I never knew why I went into care; I always thought it was because of something I had done wrong, but recently I found out it was because my stepdad was abusing his other daughter. My mum had to choose between me and him. She chose him.

I got on drugs at an incredibly early age, about ten. I started injecting heroin a couple of years later when I was a 'working girl'. The first time I did crack I was at a man's house. I told him I had a headache, and he gave me a pipe of crack and told me if I smoked it the headache would go away. It was the same man who gave me heroin a couple of weeks later.

In my teenage years I couldn't control my temper; I was angry all the time. I decided to hurt people before they could hurt me. The social services looked after me until I was 18 but after that I had no money or housing until they got me a flat. I didn't know how to look after or run my own home. I wasn't given any help; no one ever helps. I don't believe in people anymore, not even myself. Everyone who has promised me they wouldn't leave has left.

It was only a few weeks ago that I started thinking 'there's got to be a better life.' That came from almost dying and being put in a medically induced coma. It really made me think about things. I'm not talented or skilled, all I'm good at is sucking d*ck and smoking a pipe, or 'giving people a headache'. Sometimes I don't know if I want to live: some days I do, others I don't.

People judge me all the time, like when I'm off the drugs and begging, people assume it's for smack, but it's actually for a hot meal and place to lay my head for the night. I didn't choose this life. No one deserves to be treated like a dog. People look down on you because you're sat on the floor or picking tab ends from an ashtray because you've got nowt.

The people on the streets are the only family I've ever known, so it's hard to leave, but I want to.

> **It was only a few weeks ago that I started thinking 'there's got to be a better life.'**

ATKINSONS
INDEPENDENT & INDIVIDUAL

Heel Bar

NO ENTRY

EXIT ONLY

ATKINSONS

CCTV

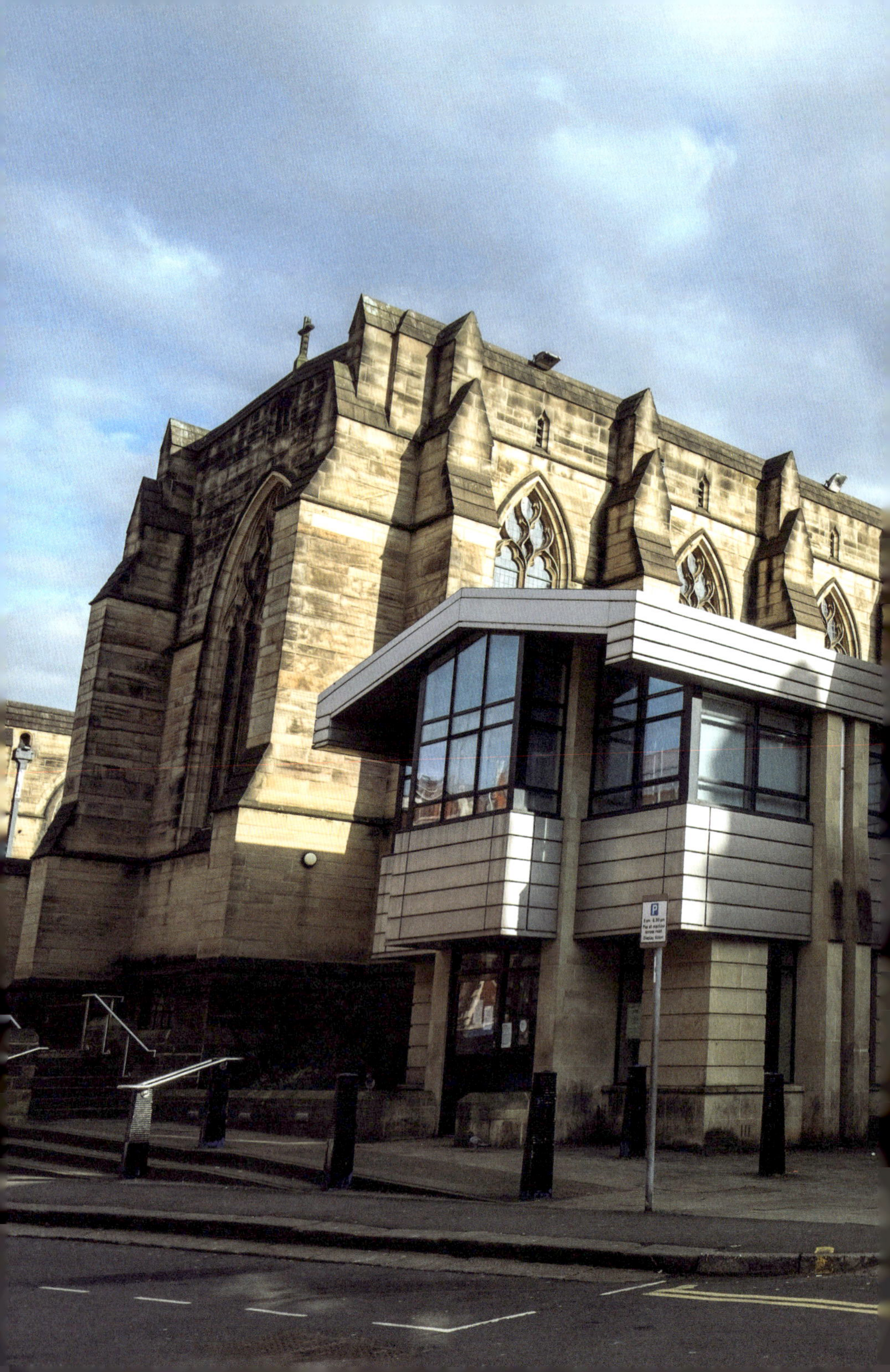
P

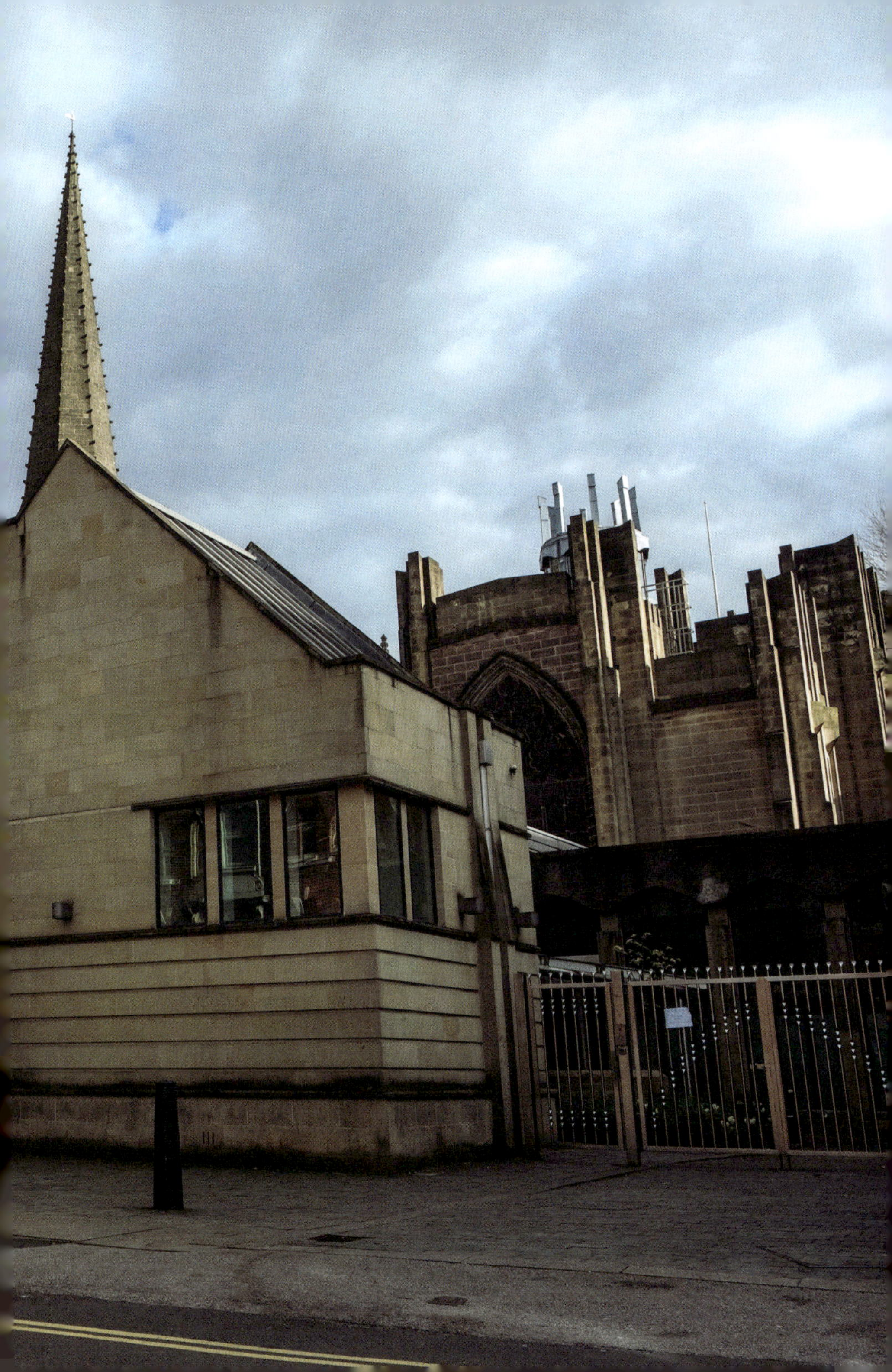

# Volunteering with The Archer Project
## By Surriya Falconer

I have been a Trustee of The Archer Project for over four years, and while of course governance is key, I feel that it's important to be on the ground too: talking to staff and other volunteers, but most of all meeting the people who use the project. To do this, I also volunteer at the project, serving breakfast on Wednesday mornings.

Although I work in communication, I was initially unsure about how to speak to people who use the project. I asked the Archer team's advice, as I wanted to chat but not to pry. As familiarity grew, short exchanges turned into longer conversations and sometimes people I meet will share their experiences. The key is for them to know there will be no judgement, so I just listen. I have made mistakes over the years though. One guy was being picky about what he wanted for breakfast and changed his mind about three times. This is not an issue – everyone has their likes and dislikes – and that one meal was probably the only time in a typical day that he had a choice of food. I served what I thought was his final choice, but he was unhappy, became irritated and walked off. I quipped "glad to be of service to you," trying to be funny. Some people laughed but another man who was present took offence and started yelling at me, criticising my attitude and saying how badly I'd treated this other guy. I felt mortified and ashamed, as if I'd really let that guy and the project down. However, the team were great. I apologised to the man who harangued me and explained that it was not my intention to offend, just a very poor attempt at some humour. He finally accepted my apology. What I learnt was that it's about understanding the place that all these people are in and accepting that their reactions might therefore be a culmination of frustration, rejection, and prejudice.

That was a few years ago, and while there have been some sticky moments when someone wants to let off steam, I know not to take it personally. I try to put a smile on people's faces, if possible, by being upbeat and pleased to meet everyone – because I am. And if someone wants a well-done fried egg, or that piece of crispy bacon and just three baked beans, I'll make it for them: why not!

This is the first stage – engagement – which establishes some trust and a safe place for those in the most need. The project is somewhere they can be angry and upset, as they are most likely experiencing trauma and potentially at their lowest ebb. That said, there are kitchen rules too: having respect for each other and being tidy. No one is allowed in under any sort of influence and violence is not tolerated. Once we have established some rapport, then the experienced team can try and move that person into a state of stability where they can reengage with the world to better their life.

So, I volunteer, attend committee meetings, and fundraise, knowing as we help one person another will inevitably turn up. I meet such a range of people who may be sad, angry, and lacking hope, but then I also see those who have come through the project, now volunteering themselves and enjoying life. Their experiences are so far from my life in some ways, but from the personal stories I have heard of where their lives once were, the other side of the breakfast counter seems much closer. The Archer Project keeps my feet firmly on the ground.

CATERING HYGIENE
Recommended Food Safety Temperatures
FOOD DELIVERIES
FOOD STORAGE

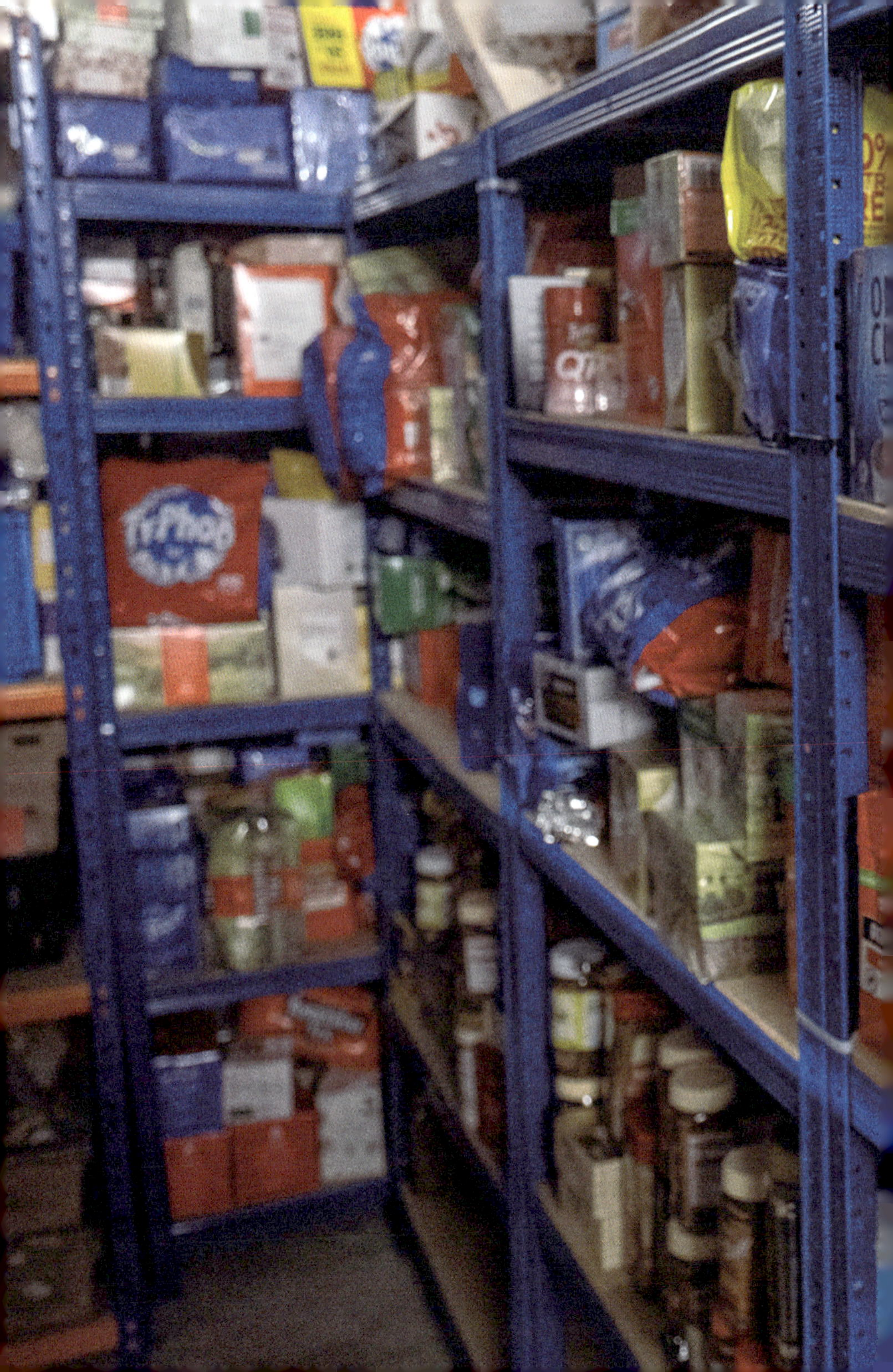

Ty.Phoo
ONE CUP
PERFECTLY MEASURED
FOIL FRESH TEABAGS 100
TEA
RED LABEL

# Better Together
# By Tim Renshaw

Anthony, a former rough sleeper, asked if he could share his story at The Archer Project's annual Carol Service. Sheffield Cathedral was full; he walked to the lectern and began.

"I got to the point when I knew I'd had enough, and I had to face the fact that life had to change or I wouldn't survive. I went down to Sidney Street and started to work with a drugs worker. Then I went to Housing Solutions. That started me on a journey and eventually, I got my own flat. It was scary. I needed help to get some stuff for it.

I was lucky. I didn't like going out once I was in for the day, but I kept coming to The Archer Project because they were talking about starting some work programmes and I needed something like that. The thing I did go out for was the 12-step meeting. I don't think I'd be here today without it, especially the support of my sponsor. But I am.

I sat down one day to get in touch with my dad. I had his email address, but I'd only ever used it to ask for money and stuff. Now I just wanted to see if he'd meet me. It's the hardest email I've ever written and without Terry at The Archer Project, I don't think I'd have finished it or pressed send, but I did. Time ate me up waiting for a response, but it came and we met. We chose a place that wasn't my home or his so we could both could walk away, and Terry supported me to get there and was there on the phone afterwards.

It all sounds straightforward, but it has been anything but that. And now I've met the most beautiful woman in the world, I'm going to be a dad and life couldn't be better."

He sat down and at the end of the service people went to him, some touched deeply by his story, and congratulated him. The congratulations were well deserved. He had made that journey. He had done the hard work, day by day.

I had listened with a smile on my face because he communicated with ease the complexity of the journey he had made. It had involved treatment services, housing services, nurses and GPs, and the DWP as well as voluntary services like The Archer Project, Alcoholics Anonymous and Narcotics Anonymous. More than that, the services were aware of the role other services played and they spoke to each other, not all at the same time but in a more nuanced, person-centred way.

Anthony didn't really think of these as services, though. They were people. It was Terry and Martin, Jasmine, Harry and Dr Smith because to be truly effective that support has to be personalised. In the end it isn't the service that helps change lives, it's the individual who represents the service and who is seen as trustworthy, kind and good.

The Archer Project by itself can't change lives but it continues to be an effective point of change because of the wider network of services it is a part of. Of course, we don't change lives but instead support people who do the real work of changing their own lives.

Occasionally, I hear people say that there are too many services, but usually I only hear that from people who are looking in from the outside and want to make sense of the process. I think they want it to be a bit like a map of the London Underground which tells you the order of the stops you will make and the connections that are possible at some of those stops.

Anthony needed some services and not others. To make things work, he needed to choose the order in which he engaged with the services he thought would help him, and he needed the process to be simple and clear but flexible. Like most people who have spent time homeless, his confidence in himself and the system was very low. The last thing he needed was something like my experience a few years ago of collecting tickets for a football match. I had arrived early at the football ground and went to the ticket collection point. There was no queue, but the steward insisted I follow the queueing system instead of walking to the ticket window two metres away. I looked askance, asked him if he was serious, pointed out the ridiculousness of his request but still had to walk 25 metres away to then walk back through the little maze of webbing that marked the official route. I hope I remained polite, but I can't vouch for that. I'm a reasonably confident person and I was determined to get my tickets. If Anthony had been faced with a similar system, maybe he would have turned away. Maybe he would have lost his temper and ended up labelled as aggressive or threatening.

Instead of a London Underground map, a better picture would be that of an ecosystem. Different services enabling and complementing other services. There is a relational and self-selective element to an ecosystem. You belong because there is a natural relationship between you and those around you. Homelessness relates to health, housing, drug treatment, domestic violence, probation and many others. Working together brings better results.

For Anthony, his involvement started with getting food and his laundry done at The Archer Project, where those simple activities provided the fertile ground for building trust. As trust grew, he depended on people like Terry to help him contact and work with housing and drug treatment services. The human face made it possible. Not every part of the ecosystem is needed by every person who is trying to move away from homelessness. Anthony didn't need the support of domestic violence services, mental health services or the rough sleeper outreach team (he was sofa surfing at the time), but others do, and without them many people would remain homeless, feeling stranded, for much longer.

Is our ecosystem perfect? No, definitely not. And rough sleepers still find it difficult to navigate at times. But we believe it is constantly developing. It is made better by people like Anthony being involved in the way it works, giving feedback and working on committees to improve the way we do things and support more people to change their lives for the better.

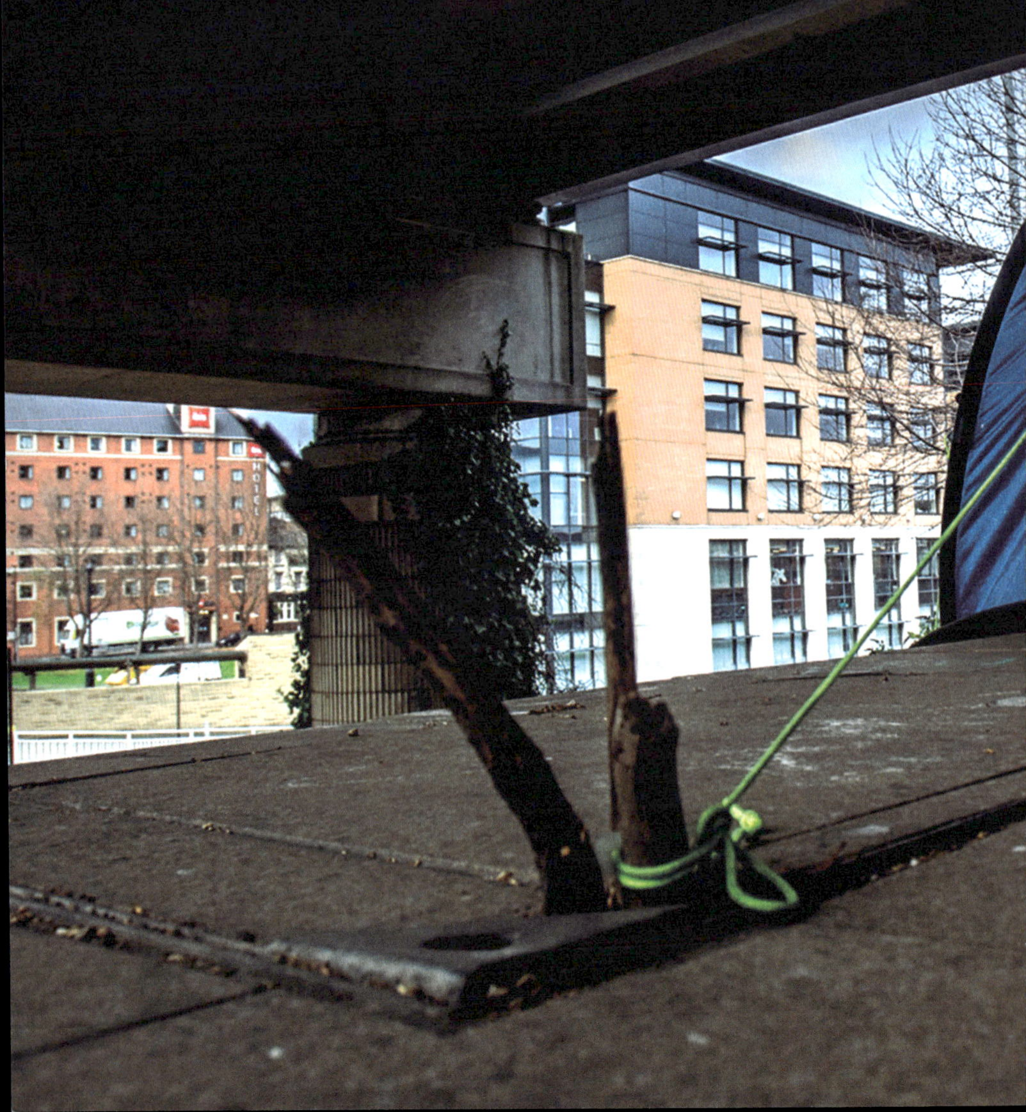
HOTEL

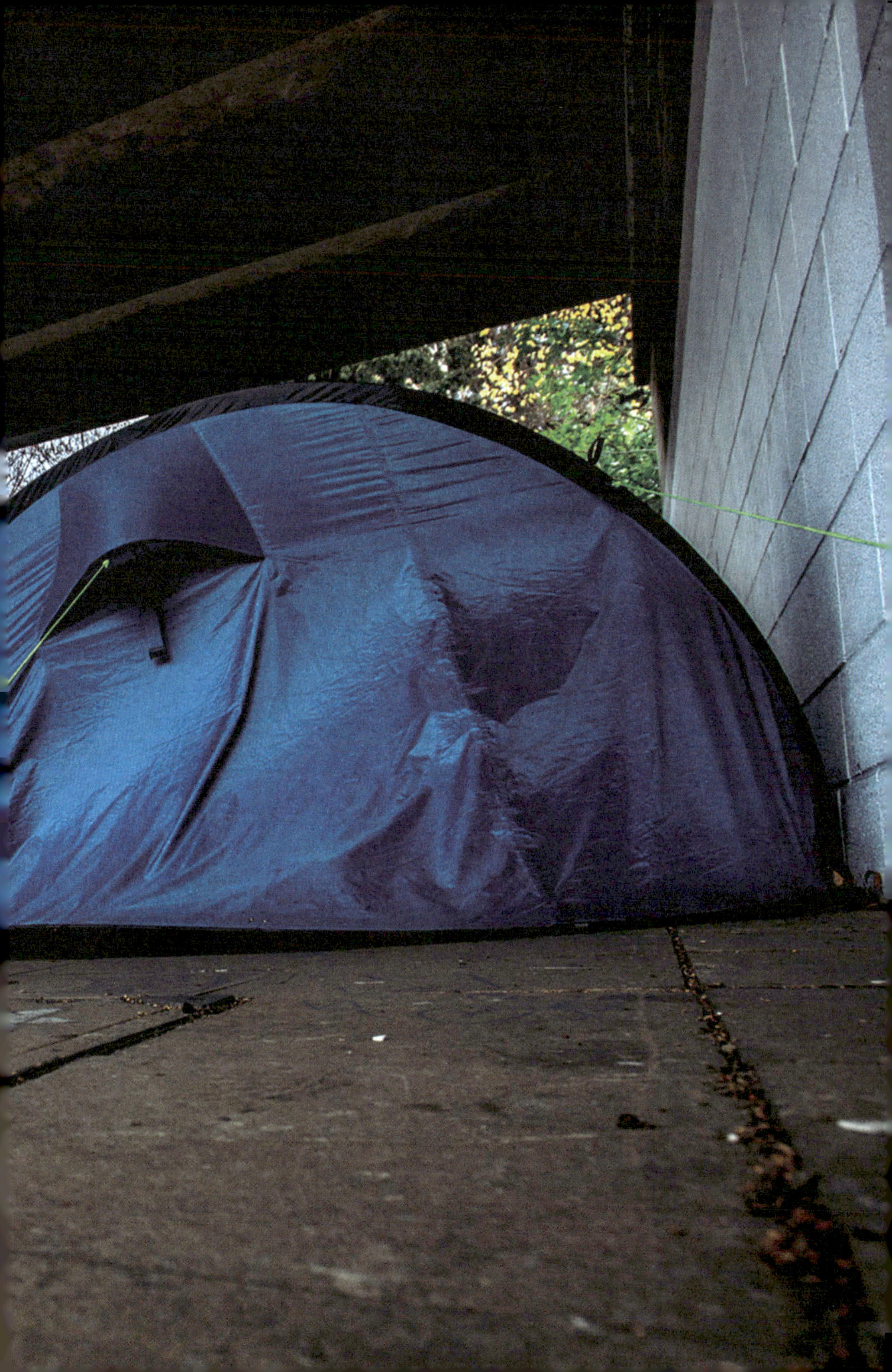

# Acknowledgements

The 14 nights wouldn't have happened as they did if Richard – whose idea it originally was – had remained well, so, strangely, we have to thank him for being too unwell to make the journey. It left Tim to do it by himself and to realise the loneliness and isolation that the street can bring. A genuine and heartfelt thank you to Richard.

Each night had been planned at a church with the chance to speak about the reality of homelessness, meaning that Tim crossed east to west and north to south of the city, taking in the different socio-economic parts of Sheffield. A big thank you to all those who made that journey possible including Revd Sue Williams, Revd Sybille Batten, Steve Adams, Ron Evans, Colin Kieron, Keith Brook, Jenny Whittacker, Revd Gary Schofield, Pam Taylor, Val Dixon, Dr John Cornell, Revd Ian Lucraft, Merlyn Wiles, Revd Mike Gilbert, Revd Matt Wood, Collette Dukes, and Revd Dr Matthew Rhodes. Many more people helped Tim and we are grateful for the support of each and every one.

On the way round, the support of colleagues Amy Rotherham and Emily Kilham-Heeks to coordinate the blogs was essential. Just as important was The Archer Project team, in particular Jo Parnell who contacted Tim every evening and morning to check he was still alive and well. The 14 nights reflected the determination of the staff, volunteers and trustees to talk about and tackle the issue of homelessness. Everyone plays their part in changing the way people who find themselves homeless are perceived and treated. Without them there would be no story to tell.

During the 14 nights, Tim was aware of the countless stories told to him over 18 years of working at The Archer Project. Those stories provided lenses through which he looked at the world and which helped to guide his decision making. It seems so obvious that it might not need to be said, but it is the people who have experienced homelessness who need the biggest acknowledgement. Some have contributed to this book and share in its authorship; thank you to James Creed-Gosling, Jo Leeming, Andrea Fowler, Chris Lynam, Richard Allen, Szymon Slotwinski and Carrie, and to all those with lived experience of homelessness who are the reason for and the real voice of this book.

A few of those who followed the blogs were instrumental in them becoming a book. Andy Kershaw was the loudest voice and the one who advised Tim that his selfies would improve if he didn't look directly at the camera lens. Thank you to Andy and all the others for their encouragement.

The team at Meze Publishing have been wonderful, putting together a picture of what the book might be, bearing with us as we made up our minds and urging us on to keep to deadlines when the business of running The Archer Project inhibited progress. Thank you to Dan Laver for the initial meetings before he left for new pastures, to Emma Toogood for her persistence and friendliness, to Katie Fisher for editing and advising on the content so efficiently and being so patient, and to Paul Cocker for the designs.

Mark Harvey (ID8Photography) has been a long-term friend of The Archer Project and has photographed many key moments, developing strong supportive relationships with people who lived on the street, and we are indebted to him for granting us access to his catalogue of images.

Somewhat ironically, Tim couldn't have done the 14 nights without the support of his family. He wishes to thank them for playing that important role of being the ones he could offload to when he felt alone and lost, and when the question of why people suffer life on the streets overwhelmed him. Thank you to Lynda, his wife, for telling him to carry on when he couldn't see the point of doing so.

Finally, The Archer Project is local to Sheffield but in every town and city there are similar projects and teams tackling the same issues, supporting people who in other circumstances and with other personal histories would be excelling in society rather than just surviving. They do fantastic work and without them, lives that have been transformed would probably have been lost. "Without you, I'd be dead or in prison" has been said to us at The Archer Project many times, and that applies equally to the many similar organisations across the country.

You Can Eat

Karaoke  A La Carte  World Buffet

If you want to know more about changing the lives of people who are homeless, visit our website: www.archerproject.org.uk

Donate to The Archer Project here:

SCAN ME